THE LAST GOOD HEIST

The Last Good Heist

*The Inside Story of the Biggest Single Payday
in the Criminal History of the Northeast*

Tim White, Randall Richard,
and Wayne Worcester

Globe
Pequot

Guilford, Connecticut

For Jack White

Globe
Pequot

An imprint of Rowman & Littlefield

Distributed by NATIONAL BOOK NETWORK

British Library Cataloguing in Publication Information Available

Library of Congress Cataloging-in-Publication Data Available

ISBN 978-1-4930-0959-6 (paperback)
ISBN 978-1-4930-2330-1 (e-book)

♾™ The paper used in this publication meets the minimum requirements of American National Standard for Information Sciences—Permanence of Paper for Printed Library Materials, ANSI/NISO Z39.48-1992.

CHAPTER 1

THE REPORTER IS RIGHT ON TIME FOR THE EARLY COPS SHIFT, THE city-staff rotation that runs from 3 p.m. to 11 p.m. He's sweaty and fidgeting in his buttoned-down blue shirt. He loosens his necktie and waits for the city editor to put down the telephone. The reporter minds the heat, and this is a bad stretch. Temperatures are in the mid-90s again, the sun blinding, the air heavy enough to cut, and the newsroom of Rhode Island's *Providence Journal* and *Evening Bulletin* has no air-conditioning; at 75 Fountain St., the only concession to employee comfort is a huge, indestructible fan of heavy black metal. The thing looms over row upon row of reporters' desks and has three speeds; two are inadequate, and the third is unusable because it blows paper everywhere.

The new IBM Selectrics poked up from the wells of desks built for old gray Underwoods, and all around the city editor, police- and fire-scanning radios bark in discord. Teletype machines pound out wire-service stories in contrary, staccato rhythms. The air is a mix of cigarette smoke and funk tainted by ink and lead fumes seeping from the adjacent composing room. In there, behind two swinging doors, rows of huge noisy linotype machines turn reporters' timeless prose into pages of lead. By deadline they will be carted off to the press room deep in the bowels of the old, red-brick building and bolted to huge presses, inked, run off by the tens of thousands, and collated into the first of tomorrow morning's editions. When the presses start up, the lights always dim for a split second, and you can feel the thrum of their power through the soles of your feet.

I

This is 1975—August 14, to be exact. The Vietnam War ended three-and-a-half months ago. President Richard M. Nixon has resigned, but his Watergate scandal still hangs like a shroud. President Gerald R. Ford is in charge; Chevy Chase is making riotous fun of him on a new television show called *Saturday Night Live*. The Beatles are yesterday, but our pants are still flared, hair is shaggy, skirts are long or short and worn with peasant blouses and long vests. Marijuana is recreational. We have mantras and think mood rings and pet rocks are fascinating. *Jaws* hits the big screen and we shy from the beach. Elvis is a bloated shadow of himself, but he still draws crowds in Las Vegas. We get our music from vinyl discs, radio, and cassette tapes. Nobody knows what a cell phone is. Security cameras are so rare as to be insignificant. Cable is a type of stitch in a sweater or something that holds up a bridge. The Internet's forerunner is barely a fetus in a California laboratory. We get our news from radio and CBS, NBC, and ABC television, and they get most of it from newspapers.

Everybody reads newspapers. Everybody. And in Rhode Island, the family-owned *Journal-Bulletin* is the primary source of all news. Six regional morning editions, another five in the afternoon. That's Monday through Friday. There are Saturday editions too, and the Sunday entries are fat enough to cause back strain, you carry too many at once. The reporters work hard and long to keep them filled with news. The result is that the newspaper has better market penetration than organized crime, and that's saying something, because for two decades Providence has been the seat of *La Cosa Nostra* in New England and home to the ruthless crime family of Raymond L. S. Patriarca.

Until last year, the titular head of the city since 1964 was Mayor Joseph A. Doorley Jr., an old-school machine politician and a throwback to decades of Irish rule. That changed when a bright young crime-busting reformer named Vincent A. "Buddy" Cianci Jr. was elected mayor. He grew up in Providence and loves its people and their neighborhoods. As a special assistant attorney general, he even tried to put Patriarca behind bars, and now he has emerged as a hope for the city's rebirth. But no matter who reigns, the Mafia rules.

Patriarca's name alone means patriarch, but he is so much more. He is *Il Padrino*, The Godfather, the man who ruthlessly controls all organized crime in New England, and he has since the early 1950s, when he wrested power from Irish mobsters. He used the most traditional of tools—murder—and shifted control south to his office in Providence, leaving an underling behind to oversee Boston and territories north.

Physically, Patriarca isn't a big man, about five feet, seven inches, but he doesn't have to be big. He is tough, powerful, smart, and unforgiving. He also is respected by the bigger, more powerful crime families in New York. Sometimes he loans them his pet hit men as a favor. Sometimes they call on him to negotiate peace between warring factions. On his own turf there is no negotiating. His word is law.

In the mid-1960s, well after Patriarca assumed control, Boston's murderous Irish gangs renewed their infighting. They were drawing undue public attention and interfering with Mafia commerce, so *Il Padrino* declared martial law; a couple of corpses later, a semblance of peace was restored.

The FBI has tried for years to bring down Patriarca, and ranking agents in the Boston office have turned the up-and-coming leaders of Boston's notorious Winter Hill Gang—James "Whitey" Bulger and his henchman, Stephen "The Rifleman" Flemmi—into confidential informants. Like all major crooks in New England, Bulger and Flemmi do business at the Mafia's implicit behest.

The FBI's gamble is that given the thugs' tight relationship with the crime family, it is possible they can develop damning information about Patriarca's operations for federal prosecutors. In return, the Feds need only turn an unofficial blind eye to Bulger and Flemmi's criminal activity. The office's pact is hardly its first—law enforcement's need for snitches and turncoats is legendary—but this one knows no limits. The deal launches some of the most brazen, long-lasting and far-reaching corruption in the history of the FBI.

Many years from now, the arrangement will explode in scandal, but for now it is a secret and eager dance with Satan, for such is Patriarca's importance. Not for nothing is his nickname "The Man." He is the deceptive embodiment of carnage, corruption, and orchestrated mayhem. Crime that is big, organized, and lurid always is presumed to be his handiwork. His very name is a kind of black magic, his influence a household whisper.

Most days he can be found at his vending machine and pinball business on Federal Hill, the city's bustling old Italian enclave. That's him there, the small man with the cigar clenched in his teeth, seated in a chair outside by the front door or inside staring out the window at a world teetering between fear of him and outright admiration. He conducts mob business from a private room in back; wise guys know it simply as "The Office."

A nouveau riche WASP couple on the city's patrician East Side—the home of Brown University, the Rhode Island School of Design, and some of the finest colonial architecture in America—recently hosted a "guinea" party, a grotesquerie for the wealthy. Smug, chauvinistic guests wore costumes that were nothing but rank mockeries of Providence's dominant Italian population. They all talked like "dis here," called each other "goombahs" and "pisans," and thought they were clever and loftily apart and therefore perfectly safe; but no one ever is, not really. It is up to Patriarca.

The Man's work keeps the state psyche ever so slightly off balance. There is no telling what to expect or when, especially for a reporter on the early cops shift. There are few places where reporting is more fun and routinely aggressive than Rhode Island in general and Providence in particular, and the reporter knows it. Anything can happen.

Journal-Bulletin reporters are the state's anointed. They are ink-stained, imperfect instruments of the community. When a busload of day-trippers breaks down en route to the Bronx Zoo in New York City, an irate passenger gets out and calls the newspaper first, the police second.

Mostly the reporters are gatekeepers of the day's information. If they don't report a thing, it may as well never have happened. That's a slippery, fragile kind of power; it has to be respected and handled with care. Hip-shooters and reporters without ethics don't last; they are found out and move on.

Those who stay joke that they're working in a kind of wild and varied theme park designed especially for them. Even the great New York columnist and author Jimmy Breslin once paid the city homage. He wrote that the best thieves in the world come from Providence because employers here have a history of underpaying their employees, so the employees have had to get good at stealing stuff.

The city editor ends his phone call, looks up at the reporter and says, "Some kind of robbery this morning at 101 Cranston Street. Hudson Fur Storage, according to the directory. The police are still there. Go see what it's all about."

The scene is about ten minutes away. The building looks out of place, a red-brick fortress tucked into a cityscape of modest old duplexes. For decades, No. 101 had been an Armenian church, but then the hurricane of 1938 destroyed its steeple. The hulk that remained was sold and eventually refurbished as a business, Hudson Fur Storage, and later, as a sideline, something called Bonded Vault.

Police are still busy inside. The reporter isn't allowed in and has to be content with interviewing people in the parking lot. It doesn't take long to put some of the facts together: seven or eight men, at least two of them armed, robbery in broad daylight, shortly after 8:00 a.m., untold valuables stolen.

Both businesses are run by the Levine brothers. Hyman is among the throng in the parking lot with his brother Matthew, who took a rare vacation this week, but returned when he learned of the robbery. The other two Levines, Abraham and Samuel, have been in the building all day.

Valuable furs haven't been touched, but the Bonded Vault operation is a wreck. It is a safe-deposit box business, and 146 boxes out of 148 of varying sizes have been ransacked. Hyman says he started the business "many, many years ago" as a kind of sideline, but Bonded Vault never advertised. A small sign in the window and word of mouth was always enough, Hyman says.

The vault's most valuable asset was also what had made it so secure for years: secrecy. Until this morning, most everyone presumed the silent alarm was intended to protect just valuable furs.

Providence Police detective Harold Brookshaw, a quiet listener with a quick smile and a good poker face, knows different. A few men in the department know about the safe-deposit box operation, he says, "but not many."

"Who rented the boxes?" the reporter asks Hyman Levine.

"Business and professional people."

"Who, for example?"

"I really can't tell you that," Hyman says. "You know, privacy is the whole point."

"How do your customers know to come here? Why not a bank?"

"Some of them get referred to us by Citizens Bank," he says.

"Really?"

"Our boxes are a lot bigger."

Matthew Levine jumps in and says Bonded Vault caters mostly to coin collectors. The parking lot, it turns out, is teeming with them. Several don't have names, or if they do, they have forgotten them; probably the heat. A couple have only first names, a surname being costly, the reporter surmises. Charlie, a cook, says he has stored his coin collection there for three or four years.

"It was nothing much," he says. "Just a little silver, you know?"

He seems awfully upset over the loss of "just a little silver," and he is not alone in that. Nearby, a short bearded man paces nervously back and forth. He says his name is Jerry.

"With a J," he says, "for Jerome."

He is annoyed and keeps looking at the front door, which is blocked by a Providence patrolman. Jerry says he has stored two sacks of silver coins and his wife's jewelry in one of the safe deposit boxes.

"Does she know about this yet?" the reporter asks.

"What?"

"Your wife. I just wondered if she knows yet that her jewelry may be gone."

"Oh. Uhm, no. I haven't told her."

The reporter tries another man, to no avail, so he shoulders his way around to a guy standing near Jerry but facing away and asks, "What did you have stored in there?"

He jerks his thumb over his shoulder toward Jerry. "Like him," he says. "Jewelry."

Jerry and Charlie both have heard Hyman say that the vault floor is strewn deep with coins.

"How am I going to be able to tell mine from anybody else's?" Jerry asks, his voice thin and plaintive.

Charlie the cook shakes his head. "Who the fuck knows? Am I right or what?"

Later the reporter overhears Jerry telling Matthew Levine that he has "over a hundred grand" in his box, which seems like an awful lot of coins. He hasn't mentioned any jewelry, so the reporter asks Matthew if he heard Jerry correctly. Matthew scowls, makes sure Jerry isn't looking, and nods.

It is nearly 5:00 p.m. when Det. Lt. Pasquale Rocchio confirms what has gradually become clear: Eight crooks and they scored big. The take, says the acting chief of Providence detectives, is easily worth a million dollars, probably more.

The estimated value of the loot hovers publicly at that level through countless news stories in the months to come. Local and state police investigators eventually increase the figure to at least four million dollars. That's what goes into the record books. Gradually, the heist fades from public memory.

In all such crimes, the value of stolen goods is tough to estimate. Any box-holders hiding ill-gotten gain turn into ghosts. They eat their losses and keep their mouths shut. If any of the police are dirty, the ranks close in around them. The tarnish remains secret. Even the steel-true, blade-straight knights of law enforcement can't be precise, whether they are local, state, or federal.

Unsavory truth needs time, and when federal and organized-crime sources confide their final estimate of the take to three reporters decades later, the figure is stunning. Not more than one million, or even four million as earlier thought, but upwards, they say, of thirty-two million, and that's in 1975—at least one hundred forty million dollars today.

The thugs escape with priceless estate jewelry, at least fourteen silver ingots, each weighing forty to fifty pounds; untold caches of pearls, emeralds, diamonds, rubies, and sapphires, sacks of silver and gold coins, negotiable bearer bonds, valuable collections of rare coins and postage stamps, and a hoard of cash in denominations ranging from banded bricks of one-thousand and five-hundred-dollar bills to armloads of piddling fives and ones.

They cram all they can into a suitcase, big satchels, and some duffels. The bags are so heavy they must be half-dragged to the crew's stolen panel van, a getaway choice perfect for its lack of side or rear windows. It's ready at the curb, waiting. The men are giddy, excited and fearful all at once. The lode they've plundered is far beyond expectation. Suddenly their prospects are unimaginable, their possibilities endless, and they can feel it deep down. Better than sex, this is.

The men leave behind nearly as much as they steal, but only because they didn't bring more bags. No matter. The plan is to bury or otherwise hide any loot that can't be easily fenced. If it's bulky or if it glitters and shines for attention . . . well, jewels may be the stuff dreams are made of, but not theirs. Cash is their god, the almighty folding green. They'll wait for the fancy goods to be fenced, turned into another big payday. That has always been the plan, to take all they can, then get gone; put serious distance between them and Providence.

The same morning at their hideout east of the city, the men make an excited, scrambling count of the stolen cash. They don't bother to count the fives and ones. That's not even chump change; one of the boxes—just one of 146 the crew ransacked—spilled out six hundred and sixty thousand dollars. For now, sixty-four thousand goes into each of eleven doubled-up, brown-paper grocery bags: eight for them, three for men in the background. Another five thousand dollars goes to a bit player.

Months pass before all of the crooks understand the consequences of what they have done. By then it's too late. The most valuable swag—the glittering hardware—has vanished, and not below ground. Some of the men are furious. Some take it in stride. All of them go low and stay that way.

Among headline-grabbing, US robberies of its time, the Bonded Vault heist has few rivals. The March 1972 theft of thirty million dollars in cash and valuables from the United California Bank of Laguna Niguel, California, comes close. But that job took place over the course of three nights, and most of the loot was quickly recovered. The Bonded Vault robbery takes less than ninety minutes, and none of the plunder is ever recovered. None. Not a diamond or a pearl. Nothing.

The Providence heist should go into the history books as faster, bigger, bolder, glitzier, and—with the probable exception of the art thefts from the Isabella Stewart Gardner Museum in Boston in 1990—among the most notorious of the century. But it has not because even today—more than 40 years on—mention of the robbery in the wrong places can stop conversation.

The heist remains a threat to some people, an embarrassment to others—even the career thug who led it, a hard guy known as "Deuce."

In the rising heat of the August morning, he walks through the front door as if he owns the joint. Minutes later he does, hostages and all. He hit Rhode Island on the run, an escaping jailbird looking for his best friend, and found himself roped into the Bonded Vault job.

By the time he knew what the gig was, he couldn't have backed out if he had wanted to. But that's Providence for you. Anything can happen in Providence.

CHAPTER 2

THE GUNMAN'S GIVEN NAME IS ROBERT J. DUSSAULT, FROM Lowell, a hardscrabble city of faded glories just up the road in Massachusetts. He stands five feet, eleven inches, but seems considerably taller. His shoulders are broad and beefy, hair black, eyes hazel and deep-set, face wide and lightly scarred on the right, nicked twice on the left. A thick mustache shades his upper lip, and his jaw is square. His knuckles are scarred and callused. His frame is tapered, hardened with purpose, and he carries himself as though balancing big chips on both shoulders.

A jailhouse cross is tattooed on his right hand, and on his right arm is a single word: "Duce." In Italian, the word is pronounced "Do CHAY," as in "Il Duce," which was Mussolini's nickname and means leader. The guy isn't big on spelling, or maybe he is and just likes the word play; whatever. Every tough guy has a street name; sometimes it's apropos of nothing, just a way to say a guy's name without announcing his real identity. More often it's because you never know who might be looking for him.

This man's friends call him Deuce. About a month before the heist, late in the afternoon of a hot and humid day in mid-July, he is drinking hard in the bar of one of Boston's oldest and most popular restaurants, Jacob Wirth on Stuart Street. He is tucked behind a far table, his back to the wall, his eyes on the front door. He is doing his best to be inconspicuous.

He has a small white business card that he has handled so much that the lawyer's name on it is barely readable. Deuce is running, and the lawyer is an important man helping to get him out of Boston and to a hideout in Rhode Island. Supposedly it will be no problem because the lawyer is said to be about as crooked as the Mafia clients he represents, but that's always the knock on defense lawyers. Still, it worries Deuce. He isn't big on trust to begin with, and he has an irrational hatred of Italians, especially the Italians in Rhode Island. Deuce believes they are the most arrogant and treacherous bastards he has ever known.

He has made his living stealing stuff whenever he feels like it while making it a point to steer clear of anything of potential interest to *La Cosa Nostra*. His vocation has earned him plenty of time in jail—off and on for about seventeen of his thirty-four years, in fact—but at least he still is in one piece. He is so institutionalized, he has never learned how to drive; all of his jobs have had a designated wheelman.

Deuce's major assets are an outdated sense of derring-do, fast hands, and a quick lip. He can out-smile and outtalk most people who get paid to do it for a living, and you'd be hard put to find a bigger or more effective liar anywhere. When it comes to old-fashioned smash-and-grab robbing, Deuce can hit a supermarket, coin shop, jewelry store, or small bank and leave minutes later with more money than most people earn in a couple of months or more. He usually goes in naked, which is to say, without a mask; eyewitnesses be damned. Deuce is fast. He has balls, and when it comes to cool during a holdup, there is ice where his blood should be.

He uses a gun only when necessary because he knows the fall for armed robbery is longer and harder than for robbery unadorned. Just as often, he can pull a quick job pretending that he's armed while hollering loud enough to frighten anyone in his way. If that doesn't work, he can usually punch and push his way in and out. The best scenario is to have a partner who is armed; let him worry about the law.

For three days Deuce holed up in a room at the Charles River Motel over on Soldiers Field Road, which was okay, because most of the time he was fucking his brains out with one of his old girlfriends.

Now that it's time to move, all he can do is stay out of sight in the bar, sit tight, and wait. He is not awfully good at it. He is uncomfortable, all twitchy inside his skin, and more than a little worried.

Deuce turns the business card over and stares at it as though the little thing has secrets to reveal. The card's face bears only the lawyer's name and a phone number. He marvels that something so little could mean so much.

Yesterday he called the number and told the lawyer he needed to meet up with his best friend, Charles "Chucky" Flynn, the sort of man you want only as a friend. Chucky is good-looking, with light brown curly hair and a soft voice that he usually keeps at a low, almost shy monotone, but his face is hard, and so are his piercing blue eyes.

Chucky is a thief and a killer, and he is explosively violent. It has long been rumored, though never proven, that years earlier, when a girlfriend sassed him in the backseat of a speeding car, he threw open the door, pushed her out, and held her by one ankle while her head bounced into pulp on the roadway. Most people doubt the grisly story. Police insist they'd know if it really happened. Regardless, Chucky benefits; he is feared all the more.

Flynn is obsessive about personal cleanliness, but his reputation links even that to his toughness. Supposedly a cooperative prison guard turned his head one evening so that Chucky could dive unseen into the back of a dump truck loaded with days-old loose garbage. The truckload of offal is a nightmare machine for Flynn, but he stays buried in it for mile after mile. The truck conveniently stops at a rest area, and Chucky climbs out. He hides in the woods, finds a stream in which to wash away the stink of garbage, and then strikes out on his own. People who know him say the tale itself is garbage.

Chucky is always well-groomed and neatly dressed, and it is well known that he washes his hands countless times a day. It also is true that when he really dislikes someone, he calls him "germy." Deuce sometimes kids Chucky about the hand-washing, tells him he's just trying to wash away the blood of people he has beaten or killed . . . but he doesn't do it often.

The lawyer Deuce called told him to call him back in the morning, so earlier today that's what Deuce did; the lawyer gave him two telephone numbers, neither of them for Chucky Flynn. Both are for John Ouimette, a garrulous, clever thug in Rhode Island who, during the long law-enforced absence of his elder and much nastier brother Gerry, is the titular head of a renegade crew of about twenty thieves, loan sharks, leg breakers, killers, and extortionists who owe their souls and a share of their substantial monthly take to the notorious Patriarca.

The Ouimettes, especially Gerry, want dearly to be legitimate *Mafiosi*, welcomed by *La Cosa Nostra* with open arms and a kiss on both cheeks while swearing *omerta*, the oath of absolute silence about the mob's affairs, even as a prayer card burns to an ember in their outstretched hands. That will never happen, no matter what they do for Patriarca's crime family. That door is forever closed because their mothers were not Italian. When the Ouimettes' story is written, it will say they were just supplicant bad guys backed by a crew of motley and feral wannabes. *Basta!*

From the motel earlier in the day, Deuce calls the first number the lawyer gave him for Ouimette. The guy who picks up immediately says, "I can't talk. This phone is bugged." Then he breaks the connection.

Deuce holds the receiver at arm's length and looks at it, mystified. He slams the phone down, muttering and cursing, and leaves the motel, walking off steam, talking to himself, trying to figure out who would be dumb enough to knowingly use a bugged phone to take a call from a runner, a fugitive, like him.

When he calms down, he goes back to the motel and calls John Ouimette again, this time at the second number the lawyer gave him. Ouimette tells him to go to Jacob Wirth's and wait. He says his cousin will pick him up in a few hours. *Could be worse*, Deuce figures. At least he wasn't told to stand outside holding a sign with his name on it.

CHAPTER 3

DEUCE IS DRINKING SEAGRAM'S 7 AND 7S, GROUSING AND CURSING to himself as the minutes slowly go by. It's late afternoon, and Jacob Wirth's is busy. The air is heady with the odor of beer and cigarette smoke and the noises drinkers make when they're having an unbridled good time. Wirth's dark mahogany bar is the longest and shiniest Deuce has ever seen, and it is crowded shoulder to shoulder—in places two-deep—with a good mix of people, suits young and old and slinky well-dressed young women. Others wear jeans and sandals; a few sport shorts and halter tops. Some in the crowd are just there for drinks. Others are waiting for a dinner table.

The gunman gets another drink and then another, grabs some food for ballast, and tries to settle in. He spends more time castigating himself for getting involved with the Italians. He is jealous of their power and control, which keeps independent crooks like him in their place, forever small-time. And though he is loath to admit it, he fears them too. He thinks he may be looking at a setup. That happens; guys end up by the side of the road with a couple of bullets in their head, if they're lucky.

Deuce is getting crocked, but he figures to hell with it. He gets another drink, decides he'd better slow down and nurse it. He looks at the lawyer's business card again, shakes his head, and thinks about how he got himself into this mess.

The card came his way months earlier when he and Chucky were jailing together at the Massachusetts State Prison in Walpole. Gerry Ouimette was there at the time. The Italians he worships refer to him as "that fucking Frenchman" but tolerate him because his gang makes such good money. When he hits Walpole, the Italians protect him for a while. Ouimette is happy until they try to shake him down for his pipeline of drugs. He needs protection fast, and Chucky Flynn steps up, Deuce by his side, though Chucky rarely needs any help in a fight.

Earlier at Walpole, Chucky was prodded into a boxing match with a notorious slab of muscle named Vincent Flemmi, brother of Stephen "The Rifleman" Flemmi. Vincent was better known by either of two nicknames: "Jimmy the Bear," because of his size and build, or "The Butcher," because he often disposed of his victims by personally cutting up their corpses. A thug named Frankie Benjamin was a good example. Flemmi killed him in 1964 and left his headless body in a car in South Boston. Police never did find Benjamin's head.

"Flynn just knocked the hell out of Jimmy the Bear," says a guy who was ringside at the time. "No problem. He just beat him up. He was faster than hell, and he hit hard. I admired Chucky Flynn because he was tough as nails and he was stand-up, but I didn't like him. He was a scary guy."

Chucky and Deuce let it be known that Ouimette isn't to be touched. Weeks later, Ouimette is transferred to the Adult Correctional Institutions, the euphemistic name for the state prison in Cranston, Rhode Island. The lawyer later visits Walpole to thank Deuce on Ouimette's behalf; that's when he leaves his business card.

In the bar, Deuce sips another 7 and 7 and laughs to himself. They're much alike in some ways, he and Chucky. Impulsive? Brave? Maybe. Depends on what you know about the two men and how generous you want to be with your adjectives. Crazy might also fit, and a psychiatrist evaluating them both might toy with words like sociopathic, psychotic, or some unique combination thereof.

Thing is, Deuce lives for a good score and the high times that follow. Chucky does too, but he has real aspirations; Deuce has none. By the late 1950s, when Chucky moves to Deuce's neighborhood from Wilmington, Massachusetts, just down the road from

Lowell, he already has a history of trouble with the law, mainly because he likes to beat and rob people. He gets much better at it in Lowell.

Chucky and Deuce are teenagers together in the city's grimy backstreets. Deuce and Chucky against the world, like brothers in arms only better, even when Deuce's own brothers sometimes join in.

Through the 1960s Chucky pretty much controls prostitution, armed robbery, gambling, extortion, and drug traffic in Lowell, and he has a reputation as a marauder. With a small crew that often includes Deuce, he pulls scores of robberies throughout the hodgepodge of cities and towns in northeastern Massachusetts and across the border into New Hampshire. The newspapers refer to Chucky as the Billy the Kid of the Merrimack Valley—successful enough as a professional gunman and crook to think he should branch out formally and bold enough to believe he can.

In May 1969 in Lawrence, Massachusetts, he and another crook raid a popular illegal dice game called barbotte, which is especially favored by Greek bookies in the area. Nearly thirty men are playing at the time. The intruders train sawed-off shot guns on the players, and Chucky orders them to drop their pants. One of the men, to the delight of his fellow gamblers, is wearing women's panties. After everyone has a good laugh, Chucky smiles and lowers and raises the barrel of his shotgun, signaling the one hapless gambler to pull up his pants.

Chucky and his friend flee with every cent of cash from the barbotte game. The heist is known for years thereafter as Chucky's Panty Raid, and it enhances his reputation for bravado. The few thousand dollars he steals from the Greeks that night isn't really the point. Chucky wants control of the barbotte games and has decided this isn't their night. Unfortunately, it isn't his either. A third man rats him out, and Chucky is sent to the state prison in Walpole on twenty counts of armed robbery. There he is reunited with Deuce.

CHAPTER 4

DEUCE IS WELL INTO HIS LIQUOR AS HE WAITS FOR HIS RIDE, AND he realizes just how much he has missed Chucky since Flynn left Walpole several months ago. He just skipped out on a furlough.

Deuce has heard through the prison grapevine that Chucky has something going in Rhode Island now, something special. It can't be special enough for Deuce. He thinks any freelance job in Rhode Island, especially anything big, is suicidal because of the bloody Italians. Chucky should know better. Hell, he *does* know better, and that's what upsets Deuce the most. He can't figure out what Chucky is up to, but he doesn't want to lose him.

They have real history together. Deuce loves Chucky; Chucky loves him back. Not like gay guys love each other, no. This is different. It's like together they're one person, and they can handle anything. Apart? Deuce gets by, but he feels aimless and sort of hollow. And Chucky? He does whatever he wants to do, whenever he wants to do it. He is addicted to gambling, in life and at the tables or the tracks. When Chucky starts to roll or bet, he can't stop; it just isn't in him, which is why Deuce also thinks Chucky can't plan for shit, can't look down the road or see around corners the way he can. Taking a job in *La Cosa Nostra*'s playground is just proof of it . . . unless Chucky is even crazier or bolder than Deuce believes.

Deuce is no paragon, but he *is* savvy. He knows enough to treat his time in jail, especially his long stretch at Walpole, as a kind of finishing school. Behind prison walls, he soaks up everything worth knowing and understanding: Show no fear. Do unto others first. Survive at all costs. Don't suck up. Don't pick fights, but never back off; and when you get a guy down, make sure he stays there. Don't threaten, just do it. Be your own man.

These are immutable facts of everyday life. They shape his world and take the cutting edge off being imprisoned. Follow the rules and you get three hot meals a day and a roof over your head for free, which is a hell of a lot better than what a lot of guys on the outside have. You want to survive, stay in line and do what the more experienced cons do. Learn from them, and when you get out you'll probably be that much better at your particular thing, whether it's robbery, theft, burglary, extortion, larceny, or murder.

That's the way it is. Who the hell ever finished a serious bit at a righteous prison and went straight for long? Nobody, that's who. You are what you are. Get used to it; then get better at it.

CHAPTER 5

Deuce is adept at robbery, but he's not exactly a public menace. Nor is he high on any agency's Most Wanted roster, but in his own grimy little sphere he does enjoy some status. Knowing that, he plays the part when he can. As kids in Lowell, his brothers tended to wear T-shirts and dungarees with the bottoms rolled into cuffs. They rolled their cigarette packs into the sleeves of their T-shirts. Deuce put his in the pocket of his sport shirt, and when he could, he wore tan chinos with creases that one of his sisters ironed sharp.

There are no such sartorial choices in prison, but Deuce still finds ways to stand apart. He not only survives jailing, he prospers, largely because he isn't afraid of it. Truth be told, he believes there are some things to like about it. There's usually a big meal on the holidays, and at Christmas there's a tree with decorations. Christmas is the best time of year, the most important time really, because despite the prison walls there's at least the sense that everyone's in the same storm-ravaged boat. That's not a familial thing, but it does make it easier to do your time.

What Deuce wants most is to steal what he wants, whenever he wants, and then have the time of his life with the profit. So he works for that, and meanwhile he makes connections inside the slam and out. You have to find something that'll keep you from going crazy in stir. You've always got to have something working.

At Walpole, Deuce joins the National Prisoners Reform Association, which is basically a union of inmate factions that keeps black, white, and brown prisoners from mingling. For a while he is an officer, but the reward for that is severely limited; and while it makes him look like as much of a solid citizen as you might hope to find in prison, the role never poses the kind of opportunity he longs for. He's a crook, plain and simple. Always was, always will be. Stealing stuff is what he was born to do. The play is the thing, after all. It's all about the action. If he can't steal something at least once in a while. . . . Well, what is he? A nobody. Worse, a sidelined nobody, and unfortunately Walpole is a trifle short of stuff worth stealing.

In early spring 1971, it dawns on Deuce that his thinking and approach may be all wrong. Innovation is the key, and the door he'll unlock with it is the 906 Stamp Club, established in 1956 for inmates who collect postage stamps as a hobby. Organized collectors in the outside world refer to the hobby behind prison walls as "penal philately," a term Deuce thinks borders on the riotously obscene. He also figures members of the 906 are washouts or sissies, which should make them ripe targets for a scam. Every year for the past several years, they've put on a stamp show, inviting the public in to see inmates' collections. Not a very big deal, but it's something that does draw a small bit of favorable attention.

After considerable thought, he sidles up to one of the many Walpole inmates nicknamed "Snake"—this one, Bill Redmond— and asks him how he'd like to be president of the stamp club. The question draws a dagger-eyed look and a threat, but Deuce persists, and by the nine o'clock headcount, Redmond is in.

Deuce develops a shrewd strategy for Snake's campaign. One afternoon, the two men inform the incumbent president of the 906 that either he announces his sudden retirement as head of the stamp club and enthusiastically nominates Redmond to be become the new president or he gets a makeshift knife in his gut. A meeting of the club is called promptly. The agenda is short, business quickly dispatched. Snake Redmond is unanimously elected club president. This is January, so why not? It's a new year, 1971. Out with the old, in with the new.

CHAPTER 6

DEUCE'S NEXT STEP IS TO STRONG-ARM THE CLUB MEMBERS INTO believing they need a master-at-arms for the sake of privacy at their meetings; not surprisingly, Deuce is a shoo-in. He and Snake Redmond spend the better part of the next few weeks poring over stamp catalogs and books about the hobby of stamp collecting.

Their inmate friends are stumped, befuddled as to why the two men have suddenly developed an interest in philately. So are Walpole staff members, but who's to question such an innocent and harmless diversion? Besides, these two guys are really enthusiastic, and the fact is, you can learn a lot from stamps. You get interested in what they depict, the country, the history, and the events they reflect, and pretty soon you want to know more. It's educational.

In late winter Deuce and Snake tell their counselors that they're so far into stamps that they want to make a big deal out of the upcoming fifteenth anniversary of collecting in prison. They've got it all planned out. The counselors are a bit skeptical, but they take the proposal to the administration and the plan gets approved.

Late in April the inmates will host an exhibit of fine stamp collections. Collectors will be invited from all over the country. The 906 Stamp Club invites collectors to bring their best to be displayed for everyone to enjoy. Collections mailed ahead to the prison will be sealed in glass display cases and kept under lock and key in a guarded room. The guys in the prison workshop will make trophies to give out as awards.

The judges will be philatelic experts from the community, and there's no shortage of them. Anything tangible can be, and is, collected by someone somewhere. And when it comes to postage stamps, collecting is one of the world's most popular hobbies. President Franklin Delano Roosevelt was famous for it. So was the late Francis Joseph Cardinal Spellman, the popular Roman Catholic prelate from Whitman, Massachusetts, not 25 miles away.

The collectors themselves are a singular lot. They spend lifetimes amassing and curating collections that are unique by virtue of the items' value, beauty, or intrinsic importance; and unless mania or rampant greed is involved, the process is rewarding. It is soothing in the way that any pleasing, repetitive action is soothing. It is uniquely personal and often private. There always is an element of romance to collecting as well, both in the artifacts themselves and in what each represents. To share a collection with a like-minded admirer is to bask in mutual attention, validation, and a kind of affection. What is collected is, in a very real sense, loved.

The exhibit will be in the auditorium on April 24. Press releases are sent out to all the newspapers in metropolitan Boston. Prominent philatelists and local and state politicians are invited. The prison administration is excited. Walpole is widely known as one of the roughest prisons in the system, and it could use some favorable notice for a change. Visitors will be served punch and hors d'oeuvres from the prison kitchen.

As the day approaches, invitation acceptances come in by the dozens; so do some stamp collections. Several of them are extensive, complete, and very valuable. As promised, they are immediately set in display cases.

As the 906's master-at-arms, Deuce himself seals off the collections in a locked room. Philatelic judges are lined up.

All is in readiness, and at the appointed hour a milling throng of guests and dignitaries passes through the doors of Walpole's auditorium for the stamp show. Collections are in cases set up on easels around the room, so it takes awhile before anyone notices just how sparse some of the displays are. A few are missing all together. Gradually murmurs of discontent turn to alarm and then insistent complaints. The crowd is ushered out. The auditorium doors are closed faster than they were opened. Prison Superintendent Robert J. Moore, having gone in a matter of moments from proud emcee and host to hapless dupe, is mortified and furious. He apologizes as fast as he can and vows he'll get to the bottom of this fiasco.

Of course he never does. Nobody does. By the time the exhibition doors open to the public, the best parts of the collections already have been carefully removed from their albums, tucked inside a crate of license plates, and shipped to the state Department of Transportation, where a friend of Deuce's pilfers the stamps.

One of the defrauded collectors is Jack Langer, a dressmaker from Rego Park in New York. His collection included United Nations stamps and famous autographs, in particular the signature of President Harry S. Truman.

"I sent that exhibit behind the Iron Curtain and got it back safely, but I haven't been able to get them back from Walpole," he tells reporters at the time.

Langer writes an angry letter to Warden Moore. "Be advised how I intend to terminate this stinking mess," he says. "I shall file a formal complaint with Gov. (Francis W.) Sargent. I shall institute legal action for recovery of the monetary value of the collection. I shall also institute criminal action if I can."

Langer even offers a reward for the return of his collection. He tries hard and long to recover his beloved stamps, but nothing works. His best efforts fail.

When the philatelic material is fenced, the return to Deuce and Snake Redmond is about six thousand dollars. The haul easily brings more than twenty thousand dollars in 1971 currency, the equivalent today of nearly $118,000.

The caper makes Deuce happy, and it takes the wobble out of his self-confidence. He can still do whatever he needs to do, even in prison. Damn! He feels better about himself. He's back on his game. What else could possibly matter?

CHAPTER 7

THESE PAST FEW YEARS, JAILING HAS GOTTEN TOUGHER AND ever more treacherous thanks to the Feds' tinkering with the con's sacred rule, the one edict that every serious crook has known, understood, and accepted ever since the very first doors slammed shut on a guy's life centuries ago, the one measure that was a simple immutable difference between life and death: You never, ever, under any circumstances, rat out another guy. Doesn't matter what he did, big crime or little crime, who was involved—man, woman, or child—or why. Every rat was punished, the sooner, the nastier, the more public, the better.

What happened was that in 1970 the government passed the Organized Crime Control Act. It used to be that if the cops collared you for something big, you stood at least a chance of being able to trade some critical information for a lesser charge, and that was that. You'd go into the system all right, but you weren't necessarily branded for the rat you really were. With the new act came the Witness Security Program, commonly known as WitSec, which went into effect in 1971. Now if you get taken down on a serious rap and you've got information the Feds really want, the authorities might not only keep you out of prison but might actually protect you, give you and your entire family a completely new identity, move you all far away, and set you up with a house, medical care, and job training so that you can start over in safety. Let bygones be bygones. All you need to do is hand them somebody or something they want more than you.

According to the US Marshals Service, between 1971 and 2015, more than 8,500 informers and 9,900 of their family members were relocated and given new identities. From a solid con's perspective, the chance you might not have to ride your own rap is a real monkey wrench in the works of what had always been a well-oiled piece of inhuman machinery. Used to be, you were more or less forced to have one or two guys you believed you could trust. Now? Forget it. If things get real bad, informing always looks like a decent way out. The result: A con can't even trust his best friend anymore. That hurts. And it's lonely, which slowly, inexorably eats you up. It's a new fact of life, courtesy of the federal government.

Deuce tells himself he is old school all the way: He would never rat, and he knows for a chiseled-in-stone, monumental goddamned fact that Chucky Flynn wouldn't either. Loyalty and respect are everything to Chucky. He'd sooner be tortured. He's said so more than once, and he's made examples of guys who betrayed him. So it pays Deuce to keep up a good front all the time he is in Walpole—a model prisoner just biding his time.

Weeks go by, then the lawyer who introduced himself earlier stops by the prison again. This time he is there to tell Deuce he will soon be paroled and sent to the Franklin County House of Correction in Greenfield, Massachusetts, to serve a few months for a previous prison escape. Deuce doesn't know what to say.

Later, Deuce shows the card to Eddie Silko, another Walpole inmate. Silko has loose ties to some of the mobsters in Providence, and when he reads the card his eyes go wide.

"You know who that is? That's the man—the main man in Rhode Island. You're in good hands now." Silko is excited. Deuce is stunned—smug and proud as hell of course. What con wouldn't be? But he's leery too. Best to let it ride, see what happens. Sure enough, three weeks later Deuce has a new home. But Greenfield's Franklin County House of Correction is like no joint he or any other stand-up con has ever been in.

CHAPTER 8

THE PRISON IS RUN BY SHERIFF CHESTER S. MARTIN, A HEAVY drinker who sees to it that rules and regulations are properly applied to most, but not all, of the prison's population. A select few answer instead to two prison veterans: Francesco "Frank" G. Campiti and his assistant, Joseph C. "Curley" Pioggia.

Campiti's longtime vocation is robbing banks and fixing local horse races. He is much better at the latter than the former, which is why he is in jail. He regularly tips Sheriff Martin to winners. In return, he enjoys a wide array of privileges.

Pioggia is doing time because he tried to make a living burning stuff. His downfall is trying to take out an entire automobile dealership, Candi Chevrolet in Wilbraham, Massachusetts.

Shortly before midnight on May 5, 1974, he climbed through a rear window of the building and splashed gasoline all over the dealership showroom and adjoining offices. He was about to set it off with what authorities are fond of calling "an infernal device"—in this case, a cardboard box packed with gunpowder and trailing a fuse—when a Wilbraham police patrolman spotted the open window while making his nightly rounds.

He walked in an instant before Pioggia could light the fuse, which is felicitous, because some of the gasoline had pooled around the guy; he probably would have gone up before the building did.

Pioggia also was blessed with political connections, so he spent a little time at Walpole and then was sent directly to Greenfield. There, he is often found seated at the prison's front desk, where a loaded pistol is kept in the top drawer.

Campiti and Pioggia come and go pretty much as they please. A county-owned pickup truck is available whenever they need it. They walk a few blocks down to Frank's Market or drive to the race track, take inmates to medical appointments and job training sessions, visit the state unemployment office, and make runs for ice cream or pizza.

Campiti regularly drives home to be with his wife in West Springfield. Prison sources quoted in the local newspaper, the *Springfield Union*, say that on some days the convicts put a hundred miles on the truck.

If a guy doing time in Greenfield needs a little distraction, it can be arranged for a woman to visit behind closed doors for a couple of hours. The girls run on the younger side, but few of the men complain.

CHAPTER 9

It doesn't take Deuce long to decide that he wouldn't dignify Greenfield's Franklin County House of Correction by calling it a prison. Compared to these punks, Deuce might as well be Al Capone. It's like living in a kind of circus and zoo all rolled into one. You could sell tickets.

There are a couple of prisoners like Deuce, guys who have been dubbed special for one reason or another. They, too, only have to stay in Frank Campiti's good graces and they have it made. Deuce is given a cell that has been converted into a plush little apartment in a private wing where he gets booze, good food, and even some occasional pussy.

But he knows he isn't really free, and he isn't secure either. He does not know what he is, and little by little, it eats at him.

Deuce has only a few weeks left to serve, when one night one of the less fortunate inmates, a convict living in a more jail-like part of the prison, escapes. Campiti quickly organizes a group of cons to search for him. More or less automatically, Deuce joins the manhunt. A few minutes into the search, he just stops, overcome with embarrassment and shame to think that he, of all people, would be trying to help return a guy to jail. He slips away from the pack, goes straight back to his concrete apartment, and locks himself in.

Deuce pours himself a jelly glass of whisky, gulps it down, pours another, tosses that down, and paces the room, his mind racing. He has let himself become a puppet in somebody's dirty little sideshow, just a goddamned puppet, that's all. And he never questioned it. He's no player. He's no player at all. He is *being* played. Like a chump. And the more he thinks about it, the more he knows he is right.

Deuce realizes that there is no way he can finish out his time in Greenfield, even if it's only a few more weeks.

A couple of days later, Campiti mentions that the warden's birthday is coming up and he wants to get him something special as a present. Deuce suggests an Oriental rug for his office. Campiti likes the idea. There is money available because he and Pioggia have been skimming from the inmates' recreation fund dues.

Deuce sees an escape opportunity in Campiti's next conjugal visit to West Springfield. Pioggia, Campiti, Deuce, and one of the guards, Russell Baird, a muscular but naive young guy, pack into the pickup truck and drop Campiti at his house in West Springfield.

While Pioggia does the rug shopping, Deuce coaxes him into letting him take Baird on a side trip. He convinces the guard that he has to take in the strip show at a popular Boston strip dive called Bachelors III, where he also can introduce him to a couple of hookers he knows. Baird agrees. With a little erotic help from his friends at the bar, Deuce quickly gets Baird drunk and dozing; he then skips out with one of the strippers.

But it has been almost three days now, and Deuce is still stuck in Boston. He has been drinking at Jacob Wirth's for more than two hours, and he's getting woozy. He also is tired of leering at the young women who come and go, and he toys briefly with the idea of trying to lure some sweet young thing to his table.

Deuce is chomping on some crackers and cheese when the restaurant loudspeaker booms over the din of the bar crowd: "Robert Dussault. Telephone call at the bar for Robert Dussault." He practically chokes on his snack. "Would Robert Dussault . . ."

The page might as well have blared, "Would the guy on the lam from prison please report to the bar."

Deuce looks all around to see if he is being watched and then sidesteps to the bar to take the page, like he's some boob in a bad comedy skit. The gunman handles the bartender's phone as if there's a burning fuse attached. He listens and says he's in the lounge.

Moments later two men come in. They look tough, and they're scanning the place as if they've been sent over from central casting: dark suits; dark eyes that see everything and show nothing because there is nothing to show. One guy looks straight at Deuce and jerks his head back toward the door and the world beyond.

Deuce mutters to himself. He's a dead man, sure as hell. It dawns on him that his new lawyer friend might not be pleased by his hasty exit from Greenfield. After all, the lawyer arranged for the transfer, and Deuce may have created a headache for him. The guy holds the door open. Deuce walks out.

The driver gets in behind the wheel of a dark sedan parked at the curb. His partner opens the front passenger-side door and asks him to get in . . . please. Deuce says he'd prefer to be in the back with no one behind him. He opens the door to the rear passenger seat, pauses, and looks at the driver, who nods.

The other man glowers at Deuce but says nothing and climbs into the front. The driver doesn't turn around. He looks at Deuce in the rearview mirror and says, "I'm Walter Ouimette."

Deuce does his best to smile. It's going to be a long ride.

CHAPTER 10

WALTER'S DARK SEDAN MAKES A DEEP-THROATED RUMBLE THAT hints at a lot of muscle. Deuce is a tough and randy thirty-five years old, and he likes cars. A lot. He warms to their flash and the shine of their chrome; he loves their power and he thinks maybe someday he might even learn to drive one. The jails he was in off and on as a youth taught him much, and the long finishing-school stretch at Walpole taught him even more, but not that.

As a more or less professional passenger, however, Deuce believes he knows a good driver when he sees one, and Walter certainly seems to qualify. The guy drives like the car is on rails. Always at the speed limit, ever so slightly over, or just a bit under. All patience and propriety. Never a turn without a proper signal. No jackrabbit starts. No hard stops. No sudden moves of any kind. Nothing whatsoever to attract attention. The guy is silk.

Deuce feels muddled by all the whisky at the bar, but it passes when he notices Walter is wearing skintight gloves of black leather, hit man classics right out of the movies.

Deuce wracks his brain for options, for anything he might try if the trip to Rhode Island starts to go wrong. On the other hand, he figures, what could go right? Rhode Island is a nightmare and Providence the dead center of it. At least Lowell and its surrounding burnouts are understandable. Prosperity came. Prosperity left. When Prosperity got to Rhode Island, it just wandered around, settled in for a time, got mugged, and never got over it.

It's not that Deuce knows much about the state firsthand. His trepidations are born mostly of hearsay and ignorance, but he knows what he knows. Period. Most people fear *La Cosa Nostra*, but there's a notorious push-pull romance to that, especially in Rhode Island. A good many people argue that Patriarca's crime family probably keeps an ugly, albeit bloody, lid on what people fear even more: random crime—violence that comes aborning, unexpected, inexplicable. That brand seems to be congenital in Rhode Island, as though it's part of the state's DNA. The place was, after all, founded by a Puritan heretic in 1636.

At every level, whether it's governance or day-to-day commerce, there always seems to be a deal to be cut or a principle to adjust in Providence. It's as though everyone is on the make. When that's the case, how can you tell who's good from who's bad?

On a sunny weekday afternoon, you can drive into a busy supermarket parking lot in a car with dented fenders and meet a fast-talking stranger with a relative who—"My hand to God"—will give you a good price at his auto body shop, no problem.

The city is known for drug traffic and its seedy population of prostitutes and transvestites, as well as for its history of nepotism, patronage, political corruption, and ethnic divisions.

Finding a woman for a quickie is no problem. You've got a night shift at a shop downtown; when work ends you're on the way to your car and a young thing appears from out of approximately nowhere and asks, "Hey, you want a date?"

In Providence poor families and panhandling homeless are numerous. Lunch downtown often means having to weave past bums, a drunk urinating in an alley, or some lost soul wearing a helmet made of tinfoil just to reach a popular sandwich shop, where you're lucky if you don't find a feather in your chicken salad sandwich.

There are people in the city you can't make up, like Anthony "Hercules" Garofalo, a gentle giant of a man blessed with extraordinary physical strength and an even better tenor voice but damned by paralyzing stage fright. When moved by spirits, however, Hercules throws, as he puts it, a fit of opera. In good weather he climbs to the top of a building or a bridge or a water storage tank and sings one aria after another until a crowd gathers. The police rarely stop him, though they often charge him with trespass and disturbing the peace. Hercules usually sings until he draws the attention of a reporter, preferably one he already knows.

Near the hard heart of downtown one morning, a young man walks by a barber's tiny storefront. He goes by once, twice, and then again. This time, he opens the door and takes a seat. An instant later he grabs a pair of expensive scissors off the nearest shelf and runs out the door. The barber, whose name is Harry, is tight on his heels. He chases the theif down Washington Street to the edge of Kennedy Plaza and tackles him.

"I grabs the scissors and puts them in my back pocket, and then I gets him in a headlock," Harry says. "I give him a few really good pops in the face . . . Bam . . . Bam . . . Bam, 'cause I figure he's a faggot and what's he going to do, you know? The son of a bitch.

"Him, it's drugs; somebody else, it's booze," Harry says. "You got to be a careful around here all the time. Somebody's always looking to cash in."

In the city's Department of Public Works, a couple of men are arrested for stealing hundred-pound manhole covers. A reporter braces one of the thugs on his way out of court and asks simply, "Why manhole covers?" The wise guy smiles like he's just been asked the dumbest question ever and says, "Hey, you never know when you're going to need one."

Another DPW employee got arrested and charged with stealing a huge backhoe from the city—but only years after he committed the crime. The equipment was brightly colored, about half the size of a school bus, and marked clearly as city property, and it sat uncovered behind his house in his postage stamp of a backyard. The guy didn't get caught until the machine broke down and he tried to order a new part from the city.

Arson is damned near a cottage industry. The number of fires attributed to electrical malfunctions would make you think there's not a competent electrician in the state.

And on the night before the Fourth of July every year, forget it. Vandals play a nasty game, a kind of patriotic Devil's Night. Fire departments in surrounding suburbs are routinely sent to back up Providence firefighters battling blazes in abandoned buildings.

On the face of it, Providence ought to be the kind of place built especially for a guy like Deuce, but he knows that's not the case. Unless you're a connected guy, doing anything there is like trying to run on quicksand.

Deuce continues to muse, but the minutes pass like hours; somewhere in the early evening darkness on the Massachusetts Turnpike, the uneasy silence inside the car, the drone of its big engine, and the fallout from the whisky all catch up to him. Against his will, he dozes off.

Walter's car is glued to the road, moving through traffic as surely and steadily as a snake through tall grass.

Deuce awakes, groggy but unharmed, in Rhode Island. His escorts deliver him to an out-of-the-way ranch house at the far edge of a golf course in East Providence, where Chucky is holed up.

When the car pulls in, Chucky appears in the doorway of the house, his head of curly hair silhouetted against the light inside.

One of Chucky's hands is by his side; the other behind his back.

Deuce climbs out of the backseat and finally, but safely, sets foot on Rhode Island soil.

CHAPTER 11

CHUCKY SMILES AT DEUCE, STEPS ASIDE, CLOSES AND LOCKS THE door behind them, and then puts away the handgun he was holding behind his back. Deuce immediately feels better, safer, and more secure than he has in months.

It's always that way when he is with Chucky. He's the best of guys if he likes you, the worst of them all if he doesn't. He's looking good too—trim, not an ounce of fat. Never was much anyway, just sinew and muscle like tightly wound ropes of steel. Chucky is in such good shape, in fact, that Deuce feels self-conscious that he has developed a slight bulge at the waist. The two men make sandwiches, drink beer, and talk into the night.

Not that they have to. The kind of friends they are, two minutes and it's like they've never been apart. They're home to each other, no need to dwell. Somewhere deep inside each of them, it's always the Lowell of their youth, the late 1940s and 1950s, when the city was a hollowed-out ruin of grit, grime, and fractured dreams. They are the same age, both born in 1940, Chucky in May, five months before Deuce's October debut.

Big Irish, German, and French-Canadian families scratched out a hand-to-mouth living there in mills and foundries and when the workday was done returned to places like "The Acre," a Lower Highlands neighborhood of cramped and littered streets, chain-link fences, and apartment and tenement buildings packed so tightly that they seemed to share windows. Deuce fell from one of them when he was fifteen and his family was living on Lawrence Street. The fall was a straight thirty-foot drop to a concrete alley, but somehow he got out of it with a cut lip, cut chin, four stitches, and some leg and thigh bruises.

The feat earned him a few breathless paragraphs on the front page of the daily newspaper, the *Lowell Sun*. Deuce had been asleep at 2:00 a.m. in the bedroom he shared with his seventeen-year-old brother, Christopher, whom everyone calls Pat, his mother told police. She said Deuce had been a sleepwalker since he was five years old. She offered no explanation of why the screen had been removed from the window. She said she heard a noise, looked in the alley, and heard someone moaning.

Maybe it really did happen while Deuce was sound asleep. On the other hand, maybe he fell trying to climb into the bedroom after some night work. By fifteen, Deuce and both his brothers—Paul was the other—already had solid reputations as punks and aspiring crooks who would steal change from a blind newspaper peddler or break open the poor boxes of the local churches. The three of them would hang out and watch for delivery trucks, and as soon as the driver carried off the first load of goods on a hand-cart, the brothers would empty as much of the truck as they could carry and be gone before the driver returned.

"Deuce was the brainy one," according to Paul. "He always had a plan for how to rob a place, and it usually worked. We'd go in through a roof if we had to. Just chop a hole and drop in." They would watch the local cops making their rounds, checking doors at night to see that they were locked, then time their break-ins accordingly. Grocery stores, newsstands, service stations; everything and anything was fair game.

Even wakes.

CHAPTER 12

IN MOST ENCLAVES AT THE TIME, IT WAS CUSTOMARY TO WAKE a deceased member of the family at home and serve food and drinks to mourners who came to pay their respects. Deuce was often among them, but once in the house he'd slip upstairs and start going through closets and rifling bureau drawers.

While the mourners were downstairs, Deuce was upstairs snatching anything that could be turned into cash. His fence for as long as he was in Lowell was his sister Dorothy, or "Dot." If he could steal it, she could sell it. Deuce was closer to her than to any of his twelve other brothers and sisters or even their mother, Elizabeth. At least he thought she was his mother; she always had been sort of aloof, but he thought maybe that was the steely German in her.

In fact, Elizabeth was Deuce's grandmother. The family's own, carefully kept, handwritten genealogy records show that Barnaby and Elizabeth (Weinand) Dussault, Deuce's parents, adopted him on November 11, 1940, exactly one month after his birth.

Elizabeth's firstborn child, her eldest daughter, Elizabeth—Betty to all who knew her—was Deuce's real mother, which made the other twelve people he had embraced as his brothers and sisters actually his aunts and uncles. Every one of them had known the truth, and every one of them had kept it from him all through his boyhood.

It isn't clear how Deuce discovered that he was his own family's dirty little secret or, for that matter, precisely how much of the truth he did know. Pat says that when Deuce got wind of the truth, he immediately went to Betty for an explanation, but she refused to explain and never did. From that, Deuce drew his own unseemly conclusion; he did look very much like the rest of the men in the family, after all.

Regardless, the stories about who fathered Deuce differ radically in all but one respect: Once he loses his pedigree, he is never the same. He is the unlucky child number thirteen out of fourteen. He feels disowned by everyone, even his own mother, as though he is some pathetic, inconvenient, unwanted thing who should be thankful he wasn't just put out with the trash.

The feeling stays with him for the rest of his life. It poisons his outlook and twists his relationships, especially with women. They are lesser things to be worn on the arm, tolerated, and used as sources of pleasure, that's all.

CHAPTER 13

By the time Deuce knows he's a bastard, he has been acting the role for years. Being an outcast feels natural. He is bound to no one and no longer believes he has anything worth losing, including himself. The Gray Nuns of Ottawa who run St. Joseph's Elementary School, where Deuce is a student, do little to change his attitude.

In the Roman Catholic Church of the day, children come into the world bereft of grace and indelibly stained by original sin; Deuce understands all too well that he is the very embodiment of the fact. Little wonder that corporal punishment is common and commonly necessary: a hard maple ruler across the knuckles, a wooden clapper over the head. He learns early to swallow the pain he knows he so richly deserves. Not everyone the Gray Nuns teach becomes a thug of course, but the sackcloth-and-ashes approach probably doesn't help. Maybe it's fate, whatever that is. Maybe it's the seed from which Deuce sprouted. No matter. There's a sharp and early point at which you just are what you are.

The people Deuce identifies with are hoods, celluloid tough guys who take what they want whenever they have the urge. The actor Jimmy Cagney is his hero, the invincible tough guy. For decades to come, the famous epithet "You dirty rat" is just another way to pronounce Cagney's name. In all of his gangster movies, Cagney runs the show, talks fast, moves faster, and takes no crap from anybody, certainly no man but, above all, no woman. If need be, he slaps one around just to let her know who's boss. Cagney's gangsters live hard and high for as long as they can. When time runs out, they go down in flames, the way his cinematic mobster Cody Jarrett does in the1949 film noir classic *White Heat*, shouting, "Made it Ma! Top of the world."

"Deuce was always like that," his kid brother Paul said. "Always. In fact, he did a pretty damned good Cagney impersonation. Used to crack us up saying 'You dirty rat.' He could do the whole thing like Cagney did. But he spent money as fast he could steal it. He'd knock over a supermarket, walk away with a couple of thousand dollars, and by the third race at Rockingham, he'd be broke again. If he had money for a couple of days, he'd spend it on clothes or girls or something else. Mr. Big Shot. He was always broke, didn't matter how much he stole."

By Deuce's own estimate, between the ages of eighteen and twenty-six his vocation brought him an average of nearly one hundred thousand dollars a year, but it was hardly a precise tally because he had spent major parts of that eight-year span in Massachusetts, New Hampshire, and Rhode Island jails for larceny of one kind or another, burglaries, armed robbery, drunk and disorderly, disturbing the peace, and, in at least one instance, assault on a police officer.

Deuce's first big fall came on September 14, 1967, when he tried to organize the nearly simultaneous robbery of two banks. Because Deuce couldn't drive, the morning found his brother Paul sitting behind the wheel of a getaway car, its motor running, outside the Cupples Square Branch of the Lowell Institution for Savings. Three of their friends were inside trying to rob the bank. Deuce was on foot nearby, watching his plan unfold.

If all went well, while the police were busy interviewing customers and trying to develop leads on the robbery, the same gang of five would be only a few blocks away pulling a second job at the Bridge Street Branch of the Middlesex County National Bank.

It was not to be. The night before, someone ratted them all out. Eight policemen armed with shotguns and machine guns had both banks discreetly staked out. The bank robbery twin bill was over the instant it began.

For some reason, Deuce's brother Pat had declined an offer to join the crew on this one.

Paul, who did join, was arrested with a policeman's gun to his head but set free a couple of hours later without explanation.

Both of Deuce's brothers insist the rat was none other than the mastermind himself, Deuce, and they have stuck with their story for more than four decades.

For the remainder of their adult lives, Pat and Paul refuse to speak to each other. Privately each curses the other to damnation—largely it seems, over Deuce's pedigree, the botched Cupples Square robbery, and, ultimately, their entire family's public debacle on February 21, 1968, when the specter of brother against brother against brother packed Lowell's superior court.

CHAPTER 14

DEUCE'S TRIAL IS SCANDALOUS AND VOLATILE. FIVE POLICE officers and five spit-and-polish Massachusetts State Police troopers ring the courtroom waiting for the session to begin. An obvious armed presence in the courtroom is, by itself, enough to cause public consternation, which only fuels the tension surrounding the trial.

Five more local cops are sprinkled among the crowd in plain clothes. Under oath, Pat and Paul both identify Deuce as the brains behind the gang. He isn't really their brother anyway, they both remind reporters many years later. When Pat tells the court that he is testifying against his brother because Deuce let it be known he wanted to kill Paul for no specific reason, Deuce jumps to his feet in the prisoner's dock and screams at Pat, "You're going to kill me."

Deuce is sentenced to fifteen to thirty years in the state prison at Walpole. A few months later he is brought back to face charges in connection with nine other robberies dating back to 1966. Those proceedings don't take long either. Deuce looks at the witnesses arrayed against him and begins to sob. When his sister Louise takes the stand, he rises to his feet in tears and says, "I plead guilty. Are you going to have my mother testify against me too?" This time the sentence is ten to twelve years, to be served concurrently.

"Even with all that jail time, Deuce wasn't really what you'd call violent," Paul says, "not like some guys. Oh, he could take care of himself. You could tell that just looking at him. He had that air about him, you know? He might knock somebody around. I mean, he never took no guff from a woman, that's for sure, but he never killed anybody that I know of.

"Not like Chucky Flynn. Flynn was a mean, crazy son of a bitch. Just as soon shoot you dead as look at you." It seems that even the air around Chucky is always charged just short of crackling, but Deuce believes that's just the measure of the man, an undeniable aspect of his very presence, and he likes it. In fact, he is somewhat awed by it. Chucky was like that in Lowell. He was like that in prison. And here he is now in 1975 running his own crew out of a nondescript ranch house in East Providence, and he hasn't changed one bit. He's still one spark away from an explosion.

It's bothering Deuce more and more that even when pressed now, Chucky is vague about the Rhode Island job he has agreed to pull. Deuce questions him, and at first Chucky says he doesn't really know much about it yet, a response which has the air of bullshit about it, but Deuce lets it go.

They speak of others things, of days gone by and times yet to come, and when there's a lull in the conversation, Deuce asks again about the job at hand.

This time Chucky tells him John Ouimette says it's a really good score, maybe the haul of a lifetime.

Deuce remembers John Ouimette, but only via Chucky, who always called him "germy" and says he doesn't like the guy because he's always trying to shake his hand like it's a goddamned pump handle.

They discuss the fact that the Ouimette brothers and their gang are allowed to pull big jobs only because Patriarca wants the money they fork over every month. When Deuce tells Chucky it's the thought of working vicariously for The Man that bothers him most, Flynn brushes it off. Chucky says he wants Deuce on the job because he knows Deuce will do it right.

For Chucky to say openly that he needs Deuce for anything unlocks a soft spot in Deuce's hard little heart. Chucky seals it by telling him that if the gig is as big as he suspects, it will be his last good heist, the one that will allow Chucky to marry his girlfriend, Ellen Grace Dempsey, thirty, a slim and wiry brunette with soft eyes, a wry smile, and curly hair. Chucky loves her deeply. She is about three months pregnant, and Chucky would like for them to settle down and raise a family. He tells Deuce he's hoping to set up a small business in semiretirement—a little loan-sharking, a little bookmaking, you know, like that.

Deuce says nothing. He lights a cigarette, blows a gust of smoke from the side of his mouth. He looks away and goes silent. When he turns back to Chucky, his sigh of resignation speaks for itself.

Deuce doesn't sleep well that night. He spends most of his time tossing between the lure of a huge payday and the prospect of certain doom. Presiding over his personal phantasm is a long-fanged and ethereal specter he knows to be Raymond L. S. Patriarca.

CHAPTER 15

THE MAN'S FULL NAME IS RAYMOND LOREDA SALVATORE Patriarca. His people emigrated from small towns in the Liri River Valley of Italy, rocky sun-drenched places with musical names like Arce, Rocca d'Arce, Fontana Liri, and Isoletta, all north of Naples in the south of the country. Patriarca's closest friends call him "George," reputedly for George Raft, the famous rough-hewn actor who, with Cagney, Humphrey Bogart, and Edward G. Robinson, brought gangsters to life on the movie screens of the 1930s and 1940s. The rest of the world draws all it needs from Patriarca's first name. In hushed conversation from the time he takes power in the early 1950s until his death more than thirty years later, it is always "Raymond" this, "Raymond" that, or "He's a friend of Raymond's." No elaboration necessary.

Patriarca is not big physically; he stands just five feet, seven inches tall, but he is fearless and notoriously tough, and he backs down from no one. His father died during Prohibition, three days after his forty-eighth birthday. Raymond is sixteen, and he drifts wild despite his mother's best efforts. Within a few years he has a police record and is hiring out as a strong-arm for the unions. Gangsters take over the International Brotherhood of Teamsters, and Raymond works as a guard on shipments of bootlegged liquor. He gradually curries favor with select mobsters by hijacking liquor shipments from their rivals; some accounts also have him stealing shipments that he's supposed to be guarding.

In 1929 he becomes a "made" member of the Mafia, a status bestowed only on Italians and only for killing at the mob's behest.

By 1933 Patriarca has been busy enough in local crime—armed robbery, prostitution, extortion, and loan-sharking—for the Providence Board of Public Safety to formally identify him as "Public Enemy No. 1," but the notoriety does little to slow the silent, rapid growth of Patriarca's enterprises. He is daring, unpredictable, and ruthless. He has a reputation for greed, which makes him an exceptionally good earner. He also is shrewd. In 1938 Patriarca draws a prison sentence of up to five years for armed robbery in Massachusetts, but after only eighty-four days he is pardoned by the governor. The long public inquiry that results is scandalous. Political influence being a most valuable commodity, the furor only enhances Patriarca's prominence in the underworld.

He is even more astute when it comes to the broader affairs of *La Cosa Nostra*. The young Patriarca aligns himself with the who's who among *Mafiosi* in the Northeast—Vito Genovese, Frank Costello, and Giuseppe "Joe" Profaci, the first boss of the infamous Colombo crime family in New York. Of the five families that controlled New York, Patriarca ultimately aligns his gang with the powerful Genovese family. But respect for Patriarca's outfit from all five New York syndicates is solid; they and their capos in New England like what they see in the man from Providence.

The public, meanwhile, is blissfully unaware that there is any such thing as organized crime, let alone a commission that runs it. Fabled FBI Director J. Edgar Hoover, a national crime-busting icon from the Dustbowl Depression years of the 1930s right through the war-ravaged 1940s and on into the Cold War period, publicly scoffs at the idea that criminality can be organized, managed with deadly efficiency, and linked from one city to another from coast to coast.

Rumors to the contrary persist, thanks in part to the Federal Bureau of Narcotics, which has been quietly following the gangland and some of its key players for several years. In 1950 Sen. Estes Kefauver of Tennessee establishes a special committee to investigate organized crime in interstate commerce, but he is barely able to persuade his colleagues it is worth doing. A year's testimony follows, however, and about six hundred witnesses name the names of prominent bad guys in fourteen cities from coast to coast; that finally creates a public stir.

In New England, Patriarca is identified as "King of the Rackets," and in May 1951 the panel flatly proclaims the existence in the United States of the Italian criminal network known as the Mafia. Begrudgingly, Hoover says he will look into it. In fact, he does little for another six years.

By then Patriarca's interstate gambling network is as lucrative as it is extensive. In Washington, Sen. John L. McClellan of Arkansas finally picks up the crusade against organized crime that Kefauver began, and in 1956 he subpoenas the nation's biggest crime lords to testify. They all invoke their right under the Fifth Amendment to remain silent so as not to incriminate themselves—but not Patriarca.

Instead the tough guy from Providence sets in motion events that sear the Mafia into the public consciousness. He tells the McClellan Committee that he knows nothing about violence against his competitors, and that he launched his vending machine business years earlier with about $85,000 his late mother had stashed in a box in the cellar of their home.

Sen. John F. Kennedy of Massachusetts is a member of the committee. His brother, Robert F. Kennedy, is the panel's chief counsel, and he asks why Patriarca ever got involved in crime when all that money was just sitting in the cellar of the family home on Federal Hill.

Patriarca concedes only that he strayed a bit when he was a boy. "Why do a lot of young fellows do a lot of things when they haven't a father?" He insists that he is merely an honest businessman who has been treated as a scapegoat around Rhode Island for decades, a posture he will maintain for the rest of his life, but he is more than a little vague about his activities from 1932 to 1944. He testifies that he was a bellboy, a salesman, a restaurant counterman, and manager on Federal Hill, and then he "played the horses until 1950."

Kennedy keeps pushing him, goading him with question after question. Patriarca remains smug, defiant, but his anger mounts. He despises the Kennedy family. To him, the entire clan is a bunch of highbrow hypocrites whose history is just as soaked in bootlegged liquor and illegal activities as his own. Finally, his hatred gets the best of him, and before the hearing ends Patriarca publicly lashes out at both Kennedys. "You two don't have the brains of your retarded sister," he tells them.

In private, Bobby Kennedy vows to "get that son of a bitch," and later, when he becomes US attorney general, he tries. He has the FBI bug Patriarca's office on Atwells Avenue. The wiretap is illegal but revealing. On one of the recordings, *Il Padrino* tells his favored underling, Nicholas Bianco, "In this thing of ours (in Italian, literally, *La Cosa Nostra*), your love for your mother and father is one thing. Your love for The Family is a different kind of love."

Raymond's love of money is a different kind of love too. His greed is well known and, apocryphal or not, the stories are plentiful. One day, for example, a low-level shylock runs afoul of one of Raymond's hitters, and the killer asks Patriarca's permission to exact revenge. He tells *Il Padrino* the guy is nothing but a *strombolone*, a dick who is slow to pay and can't be trusted. Patriarca denies the request, but then a few days later he calls the mark and demands a $75,000 loan. As soon as *Il Padrino* gets the money, he summons the hitter back to his office. "I've changed my mind," he tells him. "You can kill him now."

Fear equals respect in Raymond's world, and he is so well regarded among his Mafia peers that when seemingly insoluble problems and arguments arise among New York's five powerful crime families, it is common for him to be called upon as negotiator.

On November 14, 1957, New York State Police infiltrate and expose a meeting of the country's top *Mafiosi* in the small town of Apalachin, New York. Thirteen days later, on November 27, 1957,

Hoover establishes the Top Hoodlum Program to gather his own information on organized crime.

Ironically, it takes a killer with the Genovese crime family named Joseph Valachi to finally cut through the government's bureaucratic wrangling and intransigence. In 1963 he delivers Senate testimony detailing the workings of the Mafia in America. Valachi identifies Patriarca as one of twelve men who control organized crime from coast to coast. Thereafter, Hoover's FBI officially joins the fight.

By then the entrenched crime families are prospering. In New England, Patriarca is ruthlessly solidifying his position. His competitors in the region, Irish and Italian alike, die untimely deaths. He brings in underbosses whose ties cement his relationship with the New York families and put Boston under his control.

Patriarca alone now runs all of the region's major criminal enterprises. He builds a kind of six-state conglomerate, a criminal shadow government headquartered in a pinball and vending machine company on Federal Hill, the big Italian neighborhood in Providence. His people refer to the place as simply "The Office." It is the National Cigarette Service Co. and Coin-O-Matic Distributors, a squat black-and-mint-green Art Deco storefront at 168 Atwells Avenue. From there Patriarca commands a small army of cops, city workers, politicians, and judges in every level of the state court system—all charged with keeping his underworld soldiers and henchmen out of jeopardy so that his criminal enterprise can thrive.

By the 1960s Patriarca is a millionaire many times over. He is an unseen, unrecognized shadow behind Dean Martin and Frank Sinatra's investment in Berkshire Downs, a horse racing track in Hancock, Massachusetts. Through a front man, Patriarca also owns shares in the world-famous Dunes Hotel and Casino in Las Vegas, one of the hottest spots on The Strip for decades. One of *Il Padrino*'s partners is Haiti's notorious murdering dictator, François "Papa Doc" Duvalier.

Despite Patriarca's fearsome power, he never aspires to flashy cars and big, fancy headquarters like those *pezzonovantes* in the banks and government buildings on Kennedy Plaza downtown who flaunt their importance.

Most often he can be found in The Office, casually watching the street when he isn't out back meeting with one of his *capos*. He is the square-jawed man with the cold brown eyes rimmed by baggy half-moons hinting at long nights and difficult sleep, a mouth that seems always formed into a slight sneer, a jaw that looks hard and set even from a distance, jet black hair that is thick and combed straight back.

He favors a loose-fitting cardigan sweater or a plain white shirt, dark pants, and plain dark shoes with socks of white cotton, in deference to his diabetes; unlike dark socks, they fit loosely, don't cause swelling, and make it easier to detect bleeding. Indoors or out, he usually is seen smoking, sometimes a cigarette, more often a cigar.

When the weather is good, he might be seated in a chair beside the front door. It is his world, his neighborhood, and he is comfortable in it. He certainly could not be much safer. Federal Hill crawls with spotters, guys currying favor with Patriarca by reporting the presence of strangers or anyone or anything that seems the least bit out of the ordinary.

Patriarca's associates handle their business in any of a number of social clubs sprinkled about Federal Hill. In one of them, The Acorn Social Club, at Acorn and Spruce Streets, Frank "Bobo" Marrapese shoots and kills a loose cannon of a hitter named Richard A. "Dickie" Callei and has his bullet-ridden corpse unceremoniously dumped in scrubby woodland just over the state line in Rehoboth, Massachusetts. Bobo spends about twenty-five years in prison for that one, but a good many other killers are never so unlucky; Federal Hill takes care of its own, and much more quietly whenever possible. No sense drawing attention when you don't have to.

Even when Patriarca moves to an unassuming colonial on Lancaster Street, a quiet and instantly crime-free neighborhood across the city fifteen minutes away, he is still the personification of Federal Hill.

In March 1969 he is sent to federal prison in Atlanta for five years after being convicted of conspiracy to murder Willie Marfeo, a bookie who defied him. Marfeo was slaughtered with four shotgun blasts while making a call in a telephone booth on Federal Hill. While in Atlanta, Patriarca was sentenced to ten years in prison in Rhode Island for conspiring to murder Marfeo's brother Rudolph, and his bodyguard, Anthony Melei, who were gunned down in a market on Pocasset Avenue in Providence. *Il Padrino* completes his federal sentence in Atlanta in 1973 and walks out to a standing ovation by the inmates. He is transferred to Rhode Island's state prison and is paroled on January 9, 1975.

The change of residence does nothing to diminish his influence and importance; quite the opposite, in fact. Patriarca's cellmate for much of his stay in Atlanta is William P. Grasso, a brutal thug from New Haven, Connecticut, nicknamed "The Wild Guy" for his unprovoked and unpredictable rages.

Years later Grasso tells an associate that being sent to Atlanta is the best thing that ever happened to him. He always has operated within Patriarca's purview, but in prison Grasso becomes The Man's protégé. After Grasso is released, he strong-arms his way from New Haven north through Hartford and into western Massachusetts, strengthening Patriarca's control as he goes, and before long he is serving officially as his underboss. Thus does *Il Padrino* take care of business.

No less importantly, Patriarca keeps track of the little people in his world too, the workers and tradesmen and their families. He knows who is related to whom, what they do and why. When he returns home from prison in January 1975—an early release after the key witness, John "Red" Kelley, and an FBI agent were found to have perjured themselves at trial—he is still the supreme arbiter, the wise man to whom people in his old neighborhood turn when disagreements need to be mediated or settled. He is still kind to their children. He pays for scholarships to college, even law school, because he can. If the car of a friend is stolen, he will recover it intact. He will step in to help a family through a rough spot, and always he can be counted on to console his people in their grief. None of these things he ever needed to be taught. They are the benevolent patriarch in him, the red in his blood and the marrow in his bones. As it is in his large, close-knit Italian neighborhood, so it is in *La Cosa Nostra: Mia famiglia*.

Every cop, every judge, every lawyer, every reporter outside of Patriarca's family thinks they know him, but they all are wrong. Some know him a little, and some know him a lot, but no one *truly* knows him. Patriarca's genius—and it is precisely that—is his faithfulness to his own private rules and values, and especially his penchant for unpredictability. The combination makes him unimaginably treacherous, which is why he has been able to wield enormous and deadly power so completely and effectively since 1954. Grubbers and grifters, shakedown artists and street thugs, toadying hopefuls, and small-time, non-Italian crooks like Deuce and Chucky are consigned to the far edge of Patriarca's long and ever-darkening shadow. To him they are nothing, like so many tissues. They get soiled, you throw them away.

CHAPTER 16

FROM THE DAY AFTER DEUCE ARRIVES IN EAST PROVIDENCE, Chucky's soldiers are in and out of the house killing time, in and out, chatting, in and out, looking for a breeze in the stifling heat, in and out, letting flies in, hanging around, smoking their ever-present cigarettes, dropping ashes everywhere, swilling beer, talking through mouthfuls of pretzels and potato chips, taking Deuce's measure, shaking his hand like they're wishing him well, when in fact they have no idea what to make of him.

If Chucky trusts Deuce, that has to be enough, but there's a swagger to Deuce that almost makes you want to punch him in the mouth just to find out what's real and what's show. Deuce works a room like a politician, which is an asset, because in his gut right now he's a roiling mess, but he tries not to let it show. With every member of the crew Deuce meets, he feels worse. By the end of the day he is convinced they are all losers. Worse, he feels insulted to be working with them, though he isn't sure at just what yet. He gives little thought to what the men think of him; it's just not part of his calculus.

Joe Danese, from Haverhill, Massachusetts, runs with Chucky and is a genuine tough guy, with thick, jet-black hair combed straight back. He likes Flynn and respects him. Like Deuce, he has spent nearly as much time in prison as out. Some of his friends call him "Crazy Joe" because he is unpredictable, given to startling little spur-of-the-moment escapades, outbursts of anger, and bits of mayhem.

Others know him as "Dancer," not because he's good on a ballroom floor but because there is such a spring in his step that when he walks he bobs as if to music and appears nearly a head taller than he actually is.

Danese accepts his place in the gang, and he asks for no more than to be allowed to work in Raymond's shadow. He doesn't really care whether anyone thinks he's a made guy or not. It doesn't matter. Just keep the jobs coming, is all he asks.

Deuce thinks Danese drops too many names, tries too hard to impress everybody that he's a friend of middle-echelon mobsters and made guys. Basically, Deuce dislikes Danese just for being Italian. For all Deuce knows, Danese could hate Patriarca and it wouldn't matter. He still wouldn't trust him. He would insist they were in league. To his way of thinking, it's just always that way with the goddamned Guineas.

Deuce tells jokes Joe has heard before, but the man from Haverhill is respectful; he laughs anyway.

Jake Tarzian checks in quietly. He too is from Haverhill. His voice is low, and he is strong and wiry, with a grip you wouldn't want anywhere near your neck. He was a Marine in the Korean War and has an associate's degree in mechanical engineering. His solid reputation as a neighborhood auto mechanic took a beating when he went down as a member of an interstate car theft ring. His nickname is "Snake," but that's so common, especially slithering from Walpole, that it no longer has much meaning.

CHAPTER 17

GERRY TILLINGHAST FROM PROVIDENCE STOPS BY THE HIDEOUT. He is a good-looking man, stands six feet, weighs a trim 225 pounds. His reddish-brown hair is fashionably long, and his beard and mustache are neatly kept. He has broad shoulders and big, unexpressive blue eyes. He doesn't talk much because he doesn't have to. His presence is a kind of brutality. It intrudes on the room. He's a hard guy, a bone-breaker, and, at twenty-nine, a killer working on a major league record. Tillinghast is the youngest guy in Chucky's crew and probably the meanest. Only Flynn is tougher.

Tillinghast's light specialty is shaking down unprotected bars. He'll walk in late on a busy night, quickly knock the bartender around, and beat up a few patrons. It's all very fast and, considering the violence involved, pretty damned smooth, in and out in less than two minutes—no serious injuries, no major ruckus, and no outright police attention. After one or two visits, the owners pay him not to stop by. He has done prison time for assault and battery, then a stretch for conspiracy to commit murder. Those are only the crimes he has been tagged for.

The quietest guy in the house is Tillinghast's friend, Ralph "Skippy" Byrnes. He is pleasant, friendly, well-spoken, and watchful. He's just enjoying the scene. He does not fit, to Deuce's way of thinking, and the gunman usually has a pretty good fix on such things. Chucky says Byrnes has no police record whatsoever. He's just a manic poker player who got way in over his head a few nights running at St. Pius Social Club in Cranston, across Narragansett Bay.

Two more men enter the house together. One is tall and lanky; the other is squat and shorter by almost a foot. That's Lawrence M. "Mitch" Lanoue from Woonsocket, Rhode Island—five feet four inches tall, 140 pounds, all muscle, with a crushed hat pulled down to his ears. He gives Deuce a big toothy smile and extends his right hand. At fifty-four he's the old man on the crew. He also is excitable and a bit unpredictable. He is talkative, a legitimate charmer when need be, and well-spoken, but with a thick French-Canadian accent.

Lanoue's buddy is Robert Macaskill from Waltham, Massachusetts, a decent sort, lumbering and good-natured, but standing beside Lanoue he looks like a stork, and that draws Deuce's attention immediately.

"How the hell tall are you?" Deuce asks.

"Six-three, 'bout."

"That hasn't been a problem, huh? People spotting you a mile away or something?"

"Well, my wife, she has me wear costumes."

"Costumes?"

"Yeah, so I don't get recognized, you know?"

"You mean makeup and shit?"

"Well, sort of . . . sometimes . . . yeah. And maybe a wig and a real long coat. She wanted me to wear a dress this one time, but I said no."

"Really?"

Deuce is chewing his lip to keep from bursting out in laughter.

"Yeah. That's where I draw the line. I wear a dress, she'll have me carrying a goddamned purse."

"Good point," Deuce says. "Women and accessories. You got to know when to put your foot down."

"Damned straight," Mack says.

If Deuce had a razor blade or even a dull knife, he'd open veins in both of his own arms.

He corners Chucky in the kitchen and tells him again that the whole idea is bad, that if he had tried very hard, he could not have put together a worse, more unlikely bunch of guys to pull off an important job. He is pleading, which is unseemly.

Chucky is losing patience, which is never a good thing. He says they are good men, his guys, and he owes a couple of them. As for Byrnes, Chucky says John Ouimette wants him in, so that settles it.

Deuce puts up both hands, palms outward, in surrender.

CHAPTER 18

JOHN OUIMETTE STOPS BY THE HIDEOUT AWHILE LATER. HE'S thirty-three, stands five feet seven, and weighs 160. He has a round face, is very bright, dresses well, and talks incessantly. He pumps Deuce's arm the way people do when they are too eager to please. He quickly turns to Chucky with his hand extended, but Chucky keeps his hands by his side and backs away.

"I understand," Ouimette says. "I understand. Germs and shit. No problem. Listen, guys, why don't I take you into Providence and show you the place you're going to hit? All right?"

Deuce and Flynn get in Ouimette's car, and en route Ouimette talks nonstop about the score.

The car moves slowly through a residential neighborhood of duplexes and multifamily homes and stops just in sight of the big redbrick building at 101 Cranston Street. Ouimette nods at it. The building looks a bit out of place, like a fortress, and in a sense it is.

The sign out front reads "Hudson Fur Storage." A small neon sign in the front window says "Bonded Vault," but it appears to be a reference to the fur company, not a marker for a separate business operation.

Deuce is confused. He tells Ouimette he doesn't give a rat's ass about furs; Ouimette says the furs aren't the point, that they are after the contents of about 150 big safe deposit boxes lining the walls of a room deep inside the vault where the furs are stored.

Ouimette is excited. He's talking about mountains of cash, armloads of gold and silver coins, piles and piles of very high-end jewelry, and loose pearls, diamonds, rubies, sapphires, emeralds.

There are plenty of rare postage stamps and tons of coins too. He also says there's a guy waiting to fence it, which, given the volume and quality of the loot he's describing, is bound to be a tiptoe along a razor's edge—if he's not exaggerating. Ouimette says he thinks that if it's done right, the heist will be the robbery of a lifetime.

Chucky is silent, his thin lips an unmoving line. Obviously he has heard all of this before, or they would not be there on a ride in the dark with a guy Chucky doesn't especially like, listening to him spout off about what amounts to a career thief's wet dream. It's clear to Deuce that Chucky believes Ouimette's spiel; he wants to believe him too, but doesn't quite dare.

Then come the magic words. Ouimette says the best thing of all is, the job already has Patriarca's okay. Deuce says he doesn't believe it. How could that be? Ouimette says that in January, when *Il Padrino* got out of prison after serving four years on a murder conspiracy rap, he was pissed off at his soldiers for not filling the crime family's coffers quite as high as he had expected.

Deuce is silent, thinking: A secret mob bank, as it were, and they've been given permission by its owner to loot it to their hearts' content. What's the hitch? There's got to be a hitch.

Ouimette insists there is none. He says he's got it all worked out with Patriarca's son, heir apparent Raymond "Junior" Patriarca, who has even identified a few boxes in particular that he wants hit. Ouimette says Junior has his father's okay, so think about it for a minute: Who's left for the box owners to complain to? If all their treasure was legitimate, it would not be hidden away deep inside the secret keep of an old church. It's like, if you were in the habit of snorting cocaine, would you complain to the cops that your source slipped you a bag of powdered sugar instead of the coke?

Deuce admits it all sounds good, and the more he thinks about it, the better it all sounds. Once the job is done, they're gone. Unbelievable.

Deuce says he's in, but silently he's still wondering if there isn't something fundamentally amiss with a scheme that seems ever so slightly insane on the very face of it. Patriarca can't be trusted, but if even a tenth of what Ouimette's saying is true, the heist would be worth the risk. He'd walk away with enough money to skip town forever.

Then Ouimette says that before the heist, there are a couple of things he and his brother need Deuce and Chucky and their guys to take care of.

Deuce sighs deeply, audibly. He notes that Chucky hasn't said word one on the entire run from East Providence, so he suspects Chucky knew all along that Ouimette wanted more out of them than just the heist.

Chucky is like stone. He looks straight ahead. Ouimette keeps talking. He's like some annoying machine that makes constant noise. If Deuce had his way, he would punch him in the mouth just to shut him up.

CHAPTER 19

JOHN OUIMETTE HEADS BACK TOWARD EAST PROVIDENCE, STILL talking. Now the topic is his brother. As if his passengers didn't know it already, Gerry Ouimette holds disrespect to be a capital offense. He believes that he has earned Patriarca's homage for having pumped countless thousands of dollars the old man's way via extortion, gambling, loan-sharking, and shakedown operations. There is nothing he wants more than to be acknowledged for his hard work and welcomed into *La Cosa Nostra* with open arms. He wants to be a made man. There is a glaring problem, of course: He has the wrong vowels in his last name. Behind his back the Italian wise guys refer to him as "that fucking Frenchman," and he knows it.

Gerry is doing time in "Steel City," the infamous North State wing of Rhode Island's ACI, when he brings up his displeasure to Rudy Sciarra. That's Rudolph Earl Sciarra of Johnston, Rhode Island, where he is much loved by his immediate family and known by his neighbors as a quiet and polite man.

Elsewhere, Sciarra is a legend. One of Patriarca's most reliable soldiers, his street name is "The Captain." He is a widely feared hit man, a ranking member of *La Cosa Nostra*, and he is as loyal as he is deadly. He sits at the right hand of The Godfather. From there he dispenses fear, retribution, and punishment with neither hesitation nor remorse.

Sciarra listens to Ouimette's repeated bitching about his status, while gently stroking a pet mouse that was scampering from cell to cell before he caught it. For months the hit man has cared for the rodent, feeding it, setting up a box for its home, even tucking it away in his shirt pocket to carry around the yard. He named it "Topo," an Italian word that means mouse and the namesake of the puppet Topo Gigio, frequently seen on *The Ed Sullivan Show*.

Sciarra cuts Ouimette's rant short. He holds up the mouse so that Ouimette can see it. "Oh, Topo, this is Frenchy. Say 'Hi' to the Frenchman, Topo."

Sciarra moves closer.

"Topo, Frenchy thinks he's one of us. What do you think, Topo? You think so too? You agree with the Frenchman?"

Gerry Ouimette doesn't get it. He's trying to smile, but then Sciarra hollers at the mouse. "Well, you're wrong, you dumb little shit!" And staring Ouimette in the eyes, Sciarra puts the mouse up to his mouth, sinks his teeth into its neck, rips its head off, and spits it out in Gerry's face.

Sciarra throws the dead mouse away and wipes the blood off his mouth with the back of his hand. "Frenchman," Sciarra says, "you got as much chance of being a part of us as that fuckin' mouse. You understand? You keep whining about it, you're goin' to end up just like him. I'll rip your fucking head off too. We clear on this?"

"That's the kind of thing that really hurts a guy, you know?" John says.

Chucky speaks for the first time on the trip. "Fucker deserves to get blown away," he says, his voice sounding like it's rising from a tomb. "He's overdue."

Ouimette nods and, half twisting toward the backseat where Deuce is, tells him the second thing he and Gerry want is for Deuce to rob a particular coin shop just over the state line in Massachusetts.

Deuce shrugs and nods. He has hit places like this many times.

Chucky has turned to stone again.

"Sciarra first though," Ouimette says. "Sciarra's a dead man."

CHAPTER 20

"Rudy Sciarra always had trouble with authority," says a man who grew up with him. "He had what you would call 'anger issues.'"

Sciarra went as far as the tenth grade in high school, and when he joined the US Army in 1943, he listed his occupation as "gambler." Within a year he was court-martialed for going AWOL and was jailed for six months. It was only the first of four times. In all, he served a year and eight months of what the military calls "good time," but meanwhile he earned more than two and a half years in jail. He was dishonorably discharged in January 1947.

Years later, through an attorney, Sciarra formally appealed to get his military status changed to honorably discharged, but the army wasn't having it. They don't take those things lightly.

Sciarra's war never really ended. In 1973, when "Big Vinnie" Teresa wrote his startling memoirs, *My Life in the Mafia*, he identified Sciarra as one of the men who gunned down Jackie "Mad Dog" Nazarian, one of the killers who slaughtered the notorious Murder, Inc. chieftain Albert Anastasia in the barbershop of Manhattan's Park Sheraton Hotel back in 1957. The assassination boosted Nazarian's stock, and he got to thinking he was not merely one more lethal instrument but a legitimate power unto himself. He became a serious threat to Patriarca. The threat ended in a hail of gunfire as he was leaving a craps game in Providence on January 13, 1962.

Teresa writes that Sciarra is one of several hit men to whom Patriarca pays a hefty weekly retainer. When he is not on a job,

Sciarra is free to run his own operations. One of them is an exceptionally lucrative credit card scam that defrauds American Express of a small fortune. But his primary trade is muscle and murder, and there are few better.

Ouimette might have angered a more cooperative target; killing Sciarra won't be easy. Skippy Byrnes has been following Sciarra for days, reporting his whereabouts, establishing his habits so that the crew can figure out when and where to move against him.

They settle on a muggy, moonless night in late July at The Helm, a popular restaurant in Warwick, Rhode Island, that Sciarra frequents. The four men bring enough firepower for a small war: Tillinghast with a revolver at the wheel of a stolen car; Deuce beside him, a sawed-off shotgun across his lap; in the backseat, Chucky with a 9 mm pistol and Danese with a machine gun.

They are in the restaurant parking lot. So is Sciarra. He's driving a maroon sedan, not the gold-colored car he usually drives. He's parked at the exit waiting for a break in traffic in order to leave. The men are close behind and about to leap from their car when a uniformed patrolman walks out of the Maryland Chicken Coop directly across the street. He has a cup of coffee in his hand. If the cop clears out before Sciarra can leave, the attack is on. The cruiser pulls out, but Sciarra falls in tight behind him. The would-be assassins follow, cursing.

Sciarra drives a few hundred feet down the road and then makes a sharp and fast U-turn back toward the restaurant. It's clear he knows he is being followed. Sciarra goes back to The Helm but speeds straight through the parking lot, then out again and off into the black night.

The men are confused. It's not as though they were obvious. Chucky is angry. He is starting to take Sciarra's failure to cooperate in his own untimely demise personally. Chucky, after all, has made up his mind that Sciarra will die at his hands; all that should remain is the inevitable. Tillinghast parks the car in the lot next door behind a branch of the Industrial National Bank to watch for Sciarra's car. He waits, circles around, and returns. No Sciarra.

Chucky gives Deuce his 9 mm, takes the sawed-off shotgun, and tells Tillinghast to let him and Danese out of the car. "We're going into the woods," he says. "If this guy comes back, we'll nail him. Just make the rounds."

Tillinghast and Deuce circle the block a couple of times while Chucky and Danese hide in the darkness at the edge of the woods. There's a dog tied up beside the restaurant and it barks whenever the two men move. Nothing is easy; the pair hop back into the car.

Deuce is relieved. He doesn't want any part of a murder, and with the shotgun, it would have been hard for him to miss his mark; not so with Chucky's 9 mm.

"You know where this bastard lives?" Chucky asks Tillinghast.
"Sure."

"Well," Chucky says, "we're going up there and nail this guy."

They spot Sciarra's maroon car in the driveway of his home in Johnston, but his gold-colored car is nowhere to be seen, which causes a panic. The men conclude Sciarra knows the score, has switched cars, and now, with the game playing out on his own turf, may be tracking them. The would-be assassins leave Johnston in a hurry.

CHAPTER 21

At 5 Golf Avenue the next day, they report to Ouimette that Sciarra has nine lives. Deuce figures it can't be that simple, but he shuts up. He had misgivings to begin with, and the ill-fated cat-and-mouse game at The Helm has left him queasy. There's something wrong with this whole thing, he figures. Sciarra should have been easy. Nobody gets so lucky as to have a cop just show up out of nowhere at precisely the right moment. Then minutes later, the target makes the car that's following him? Only a sucker believes in coincidence. He wishes he had stayed in his faux jail cell in Greenfield.

The crew develops a second plan to take out Sciarra. Byrnes reports that after several days of following the hit man, it is clearly Sciarra's habit to sit in the same spot at The Helm—on a stool at the end of the bar, which is near the hallway leading to the men's room. Deuce is to be the spotter. He will go to The Helm carrying two 9 mm pistols and order a meal that includes wine chilling in an ice bucket. When Sciarra shows up, Deuce will go to the pay phone and call a room at the nearby Howard Johnson's Motor Lodge, where Tillinghast, Flynn, and Danese will be waiting.

Danese will walk into The Helm and find a spot near Sciarra. Flynn will come in, the sawed-off shotgun under his jacket, go straight to the men's room, and slip on a mask and gloves. As soon as Chucky walks by, Deuce will wipe down his silverware and drop the utensils into the ice bucket. Chucky will come out of the men's room, walk up behind Sciarra, and blow his head off. Danese will kill anyone accompanying Sciarra. As the two men leave the restaurant, Deuce will cover them with his two handguns.

75

The plan might work if Sciarra shows up, but he is nowhere to be found.

The men try the same plan a couple of nights later. This time they find Sciarra, but the killer has company. He's dining with his lawyer, one of the mob's best. If he were to be collateral damage there would be hell to pay. The men turn tail. By now Deuce is convinced nothing is ever going to come of this game. Worse, it feels to him that, as complicated as it may be, the fix is in; nothing is meant to happen. It's the only thing that makes any sense, but he can't even be sure of that, so he remains uneasy.

John Ouimette tells Chucky and his crew that at 1:00 p.m. on the same day every week, Sciarra goes to Village Auto Body in Wakefield, Rhode Island, picks up a payoff, visits for a while, and then leaves. Byrnes will stake out the garage.

When Sciarra shows up, Byrnes will signal Danese, Flynn, and Deuce, who will be waiting with Tillinghast nearby. The four of them will put on masks and gloves, then two will enter the body shop from the front, two through the back, and all four men will round up the workers and any customers. They will demand money and in the course of the holdup find an excuse to shoot Sciarra.

But once again, Sciarra breaks the pattern. He didn't get to be one of *Il Padrino*'s best by being careless. He fails to show up at the garage.

The gang is incensed. The men return to the hideout in East Providence, grousing over Sciarra's good fortune and cursing their own bad luck. Deuce doesn't know what to think now. He's idly watching the evening news on television when the broadcast shows none other than Rudy Sciarra being arrested only hours earlier on a charge that he had helped plan a prisoner escape from the state prison months earlier.

The room groans in unison. Deuce shakes his head. He doesn't believe in coincidence. Hidden agendas, unseen forces, yes; but coincidence, never. He tries to chalk it all up to bad luck in a state that surely must be one of God's forsaken, but that doesn't quite work either.

CHAPTER 22

THE WOULD-BE ASSASSINS ARE LEFT FEELING PROFESSIONALLY
inadequate, impotent really, which is profoundly embarrassing to
a bunch of testosterone-twisted guys who trade in robbery and
murder. John Ouimette is angry at the failure to take down Sciarra, knowing he'll have to answer to his brother Gerry, whose
anger is certain to make his own look like a Victorian maiden's
attack of the vapors.

Time for the second favor. Ouimette gives Deuce the address
of a big coin shop just over the state line in Seekonk, Massachusetts. He believes the owner is holding a new supply of gold coins,
always an inviting prospect and the kind of job that is second
nature to Deuce; he has hit stamp and coin shops dozens of times.
He takes the lead, walks in with one of the men, pulls a gun, ties
up the employees, lets in the other crooks, and manages the store
while they loot it. It'd be different today, what with security cameras all over the place and maybe a plainclothes cop too if the
target's big enough. But in the seventies, a crook hardly needs a
plan. Just balls. No big deal.

He decides to take Macaskill, Lanoue, and Tarzian with him
because it seems to him that of all of the men in Chucky's so-
called crew, they need practice the most. They park their car at the
curb down the street.

Deuce tells Lanoue and Tarzian to give him and Macaskill
time to take the place then just wander over and he'll let them in.

Deuce and Macaskill enter the store. Deuce pulls out a handgun, and in less than a minute he and Macaskill have two employees

tied up and helpless. He hears a knock on the picture window at the front of the store and turns to find Lanoue and Tarzian standing outside with their noses pressed to the window. The weather is hot, and they have decided to wear "clever" disguises—heavy jackets and broad-brimmed hats—and they are holding folded duffle bags. Deuce is incredulous. Against his better judgment, he buzzes them into the store.

The captive employees are wide-eyed with fright. One of them stares at Lanoue, who immediately starts screaming at the man: "Don't you be eyeballing me, hey, you son of a bitch!"

He walks over to the man and starts kicking him. Deuce and Macaskill leap on Lanoue, drag him off the hapless victim, and shove him toward the vaults, which are behind heavy glass doors at the back of the store. Deuce is outraged and frustrated nearly to the point of tears.

"Get in there," he shouts. "Get the fucking coins, and let's get out of here. Now."

Minutes later, Lanoue, Tarzian, and Macaskill come out of the vaults hauling heavy bags bulging with coins. Deuce is reassuring his captives that they will be fine and that the robbery will be over in a minute when he hears a commotion.

"What the hell's wrong back there?" he barks.

Lanoue's thick French-Canadian accent answers him. "Well, if he ain't going to open the door for me, I ain't going to open the door for him, no. These bags weigh a ton."

For an instant Deuce considers calling the police; life in prison is saner than this.

"You don't get out here," he says, "I swear to God, I'll shoot you."

He glares at the three men as they drag themselves and their loot out of the store and across the sidewalk to the car waiting at the curb. Deuce turns to the bound employees, warns them not to sound an alarm for several minutes, and then shrugs with exasperation before leaving.

Outside, Lanoue and Macaskill are causing a scene—calling each other names, swearing loudly, and attracting passersby. This time they are arguing over who will sit in the front seat and who will sit in the back.

Deuce is speechless. He folds his arms, leans against the car, and practices taking deep breaths while Lanoue and Macaskill keep bickering. Finally he pushes them inside, and as they continue their argument, Deuce consoles himself with the prospect of counting the money they just stole.

They carry the bags into the hideout at 5 Golf Avenue, and Chucky opens them. When he looks up, his lips are drawn so tight they're nearly white.

"Whose job was it to fill the bags?"

Deuce points to Lanoue, who is rocking in a chair in the corner of the room. "That buffoon over there."

"Where's the gold ones?" Chucky asks. "These are just about worthless."

"Nobody said nothing about no gold coins," Lanoue sputters. "How am I supposed to know where they are?"

Lanoue had stuffed Swedish, Japanese, and Turkish coins into the bags, which might be worth a little something to collectors, but not to crooks looking for fast cash.

Chucky is so angry he can't speak. He walks out of the house.

Lanoue is angry because everyone is angry with him. He stalks out of the hideout, buys a few coin catalogs and a magnifying glass, and spends the rest of the day in the corner of the living room trying to sort out the stolen coins while pouting and muttering under his breath in two languages.

CHAPTER 23

DEUCE IS DEPRESSED. HE IS CONVINCED THAT COMING TO RHODE Island is the worst move he has made in years, and he's got a few bad ones to pick from. He's batting zero on both of the jobs he's taken. First, hitting Sciarra, though he's just as glad that didn't work out because he hasn't killed anyone before. Then there was the fiasco at the coin shop, which should have gone like clockwork.

How could he know Lanoue would blow up on him? He figures Lanoue is his biggest liability, but he sort of likes the old guy. He's funny, and he doesn't put up with much crap from anybody. Thing is, he just never seems to stay on the same track for too long, kind of flits from one thing to another, sort of in control, sort of not. So over the weekend, Deuce takes him aside and starts selling him on the notion that as driver of the getaway van, Lanoue has the key role in the heist, more important, in fact, than anybody else's.

"Everything you do," Deuce says, "is going to make the difference between us pulling off this job or getting caught with our pants down." He has Lanoue drive the route to and from Bonded Vault more than a dozen times, every time repeatedly going over the details of the guy's job.

Deuce tells him flatly and forcefully, "When everyone's in the truck, you're the boss. You call the shots. There's no talking." He reminds Lanoue to make sure the men put on their coveralls and masks before they leave the van, and he says they must walk to the building in pairs about a minute apart so as not to attract attention. He warns Lanoue to stay alert and, if he sees anything really suspicious, to come in and get him.

The getaway should be simple too. Lanoue is to help load everything into the van then drive the men to their three cars, which will have been parked nearby in different spots around the block. Then he is to drive slowly back to the hideout.

Lanoue laps it up, and Deuce is convinced the old man will be okay. With Lanoue more or less neutralized, Deuce tries to relax a little.

The next day, Monday, August 11, Ouimette stops by, tells the crew they will hit Bonded Vault first thing Wednesday morning, August 13, and gives them five hundred dollars. Deuce and Byrnes go shopping for the tools they'll need for the break-in—a few crowbars; a couple of power drills with the hardest bits available; long, heavy-duty extension cords; and sets of dark worker's coveralls. They go out of state, to stores in New London and Groton, Connecticut, figuring that by changing the venues they will throw police investigators off their scent.

Back at the hideout, Deuce fills toolboxes for the crew and goes over the plan he and Chucky came up with. He reminds everyone that if they need to speak with one another on the job, they are to use the name "Harry." That's everyone's name, "Harry." If they can shut up all together, that's even better.

Lanoue, in his stolen van, is to pick up the men as they drop off their three cars, then drive everyone to Cranston Street. He'll park the van down the road just out of sight of the building. When he sees the first of the men come out to the curb with a full bag, he will ease the vehicle up the street and stop in front of the building. Until then, Lanoue is to simply sit, watch, and wait.

On August 12, the day before the heist, Ouimette tells Flynn and Deuce the score will have to wait a day because somebody higher up the food chain needs time to get his machine gun out of one of the safe deposit boxes.

"It'd bring too much heat if it got left behind," Ouimette says.

Deuce lets loose with a string of obscenities. He doesn't believe the machine gun story. Except for Byrnes, everybody involved in the robbery has a rap sheet you could wallpaper a small room with. They get caught with cap pistols, it's all over. And now it's time to worry about a machine gun?

He figures somebody's moving valuable goods to safety. He has been on edge anyway, and now he is seething, his mind racing. He feels as though he's about to explode again when Byrnes bursts into the house.

"We just blew the truck," he announces. "We were cleaning it out, and some cop in the neighborhood spotted us standing next to it. If the cop remembers, he'll be able to make us when they find the truck after the score."

The men agree to steal a new van. The task goes to Walter Ouimette. They have to wait another day anyway, thanks to the supposed machine gun problem. As soon as everyone leaves, Deuce tries a final time to talk Chucky out of the job. He might as well have struck up a conversation with a gravestone.

Exasperated, Deuce calls a cab and announces to Chucky that he's going out to buy some Chinese chicken wings.

Thirty minutes later, at Ming Garden, a popular Chinese restaurant on Kennedy Plaza in downtown Providence, Deuce asks for a double order of chicken wings and sits down to wait. Ten minutes later, order in hand, he walks outside and signals another cab. He climbs in the back, and the taxi heads out. The muffler is loud enough to announce the Second Coming. Less than a mile from Flynn's hideout, the cab is stopped by East Providence police officers. Turns out, the taxi's taillights don't work either; the cops spotted that even before they could hear the car.

Deuce cracks open the rear door, letting out a scrumptious aroma cloud of soy and ginger. He tells the two patrolmen that if it's all the same to them, he'd just as soon walk home with his chicken wings; no hard feelings. He says his kids are waiting for him and they're hungry. He puts one foot on the pavement and starts to get out of the cab.

"Stay right there, sir," one of the cops says. "Get back in the vehicle, please."

Deuce winces but obliges.

The patrolman sneers at the cab and tells the driver curtly, "What a piece of junk. I should order you off the road."

"No," says other man, a patrol sergeant. "Just give him a citation. This guy's family's waiting for supper."

Deuce mutters his thanks to the cops. He exhales and sinks back into the car seat. He has lost his appetite. He leaves the double order of chicken wings on the kitchen table and tells Chucky he needs a good night's sleep.

"All I got to say is, if things don't go any better tomorrow, Charles, we're royally fucked."

"It'll be fine, Deuce," Chucky says. "We're going to get rich."

CHAPTER 24

AT PRECISELY 8:00 A.M. FIVE DAYS A WEEK, A STOOPED LITTLE
man named Sam Levine opens his Bonded Vault. The door to it
is a massive, foot-thick slab of molded stainless steel weighing
seven tons, fourteen thousand pounds. It would take high explo-
sives to go through it. He dials the lock combination, and perfectly
machined tumblers turn. The doors unlock. Furs worth hundreds
of thousands of dollars hang on racks inside, and just beyond is
an inner sanctum, a rectangle about the size of the average ranch
house living room. It contains about 150 safe deposit boxes of
varying sizes, most very large.

As Levine returns to his office around the corner, a dark green
panel van pulls up to the curb out of sight and down the street.
Traffic is slight. There are no pedestrians. The air in the closed van
is stifling, hot, and there's not nearly enough of it for the comfort
of eight men. Lanoue is driving. Deuce is beside him. Chucky,
Tillinghast, Danese, Tarzian, Macaskill, and Byrnes are packed in
behind them.

They have parked three cars at prearranged sites around the
block and joined everyone else in the van, so now it holds eight
men. They are in an ugly mood, nervous and growing more short-
tempered by the second. Even Deuce, though calm is what he's
paid for. He sits in relative silence, as though alone. The other men
are big or wide, some both, except for Macaskill, who is skinny and
tall. They are not built for tight places or quick wardrobe changes.
Their dark worker's coveralls, masks, and the tools they bought
with John Ouimette's five hundred dollars cover the floor.

One of the men falls into another while trying to fit into a jumpsuit. The guy responds with a hard push. One push begets another, and then another. Every move is punctuated by a loud obscenity. In moments the men are pushing and shoving each other into the walls, which makes the van rock and lurch erratically from side to side.

The fighting enrages Lanoue. He has been assured that he is the boss of the van. No talking, he had told the men; not a word, not a goddamned solitary word. And here they are, cursing and shouting and making the van jerk around like a four-wheeled advertisement for trouble.

He tries to outshout them. "Do what the hell I fucking tell you, hey."

The men decline.

"Shut the fuck up," says one.

"Yeah, you little French fuck. Who the fuck you think you are?"

"Shut the fuck up," orders another.

"Hey, you the boss now, you little shit?"

This greatly displeases Lanoue, so he shouts even louder.

"You miserable sons of bitches, you . . ."

Deuce has had enough.

"Knock it off! All of you. Jesus H. Christ! Knock it off, or I swear to God I'll kill somebody."

As far as anyone knows, Deuce has never shot anybody, nor has he killed anyone, but that doesn't mean he couldn't, and it certainly doesn't mean he wouldn't.

The men don't really give a damn. At least three of them have killed before and would again without hesitation. Two of them are especially good at it. But what they all know for sure, and not from watching B-grade movies, is that when somebody carrying a gun gets really pissed off in close quarters, there are only two choices: Kill him or do what he says. As options go, the former isn't viable, what with Deuce being Chucky's appointed leader and all, so, if only for the moment, the men quiet down.

Deuce is wishing he were safely back in prison where things are predictable enough to make uncertainty something to fear. What you don't know can kill you. In his gut, he worries that what he doesn't know about this job could turn it into a mass suicide.

He still would dearly like to leave the entire crew to its own inevitable destruction, but the prospect of a big score is just too much to pass up. Wealth trumps all. Deuce knows he is in it for the distance now. He twists halfway around in his seat and turns to Chucky. Flynn is staring straight ahead. He's wide-eyed, tight-lipped, and wound tighter than a hangman's noose.

"I'll see you in thirty seconds," Deuce says.

Chucky nods sharply just once.

Deuce moves, opens the door of the van, and steps out into the muggy heat of the August morning.

CHAPTER 25

CRANSTON STREET IS STILL QUIET. DEUCE TRIES TO ROLL THE tension out of his shoulders. He rocks his head from side to side, like a boxer loosening up. From behind blue-tinted sunglasses, he surveys the street then walks straight toward Bonded Vault. He's wearing a new light-gray suit and carrying a leather valise under his right arm, tightly, because the revolver Chucky gave him is inside. Deuce doesn't look threatening, just intent, all business; but as he walks toward the building, he is nervous, his mind racing, running through everything that has brought him to this, the unlikeliest of places, looking to score big.

He's thinking that maybe, just maybe, this is *the* job, the one every crook longs for but never gets. His mind races. What if . . . ? What if, when all is said and done, he has been born just for this one gig and it turns out to be gigantic? Why not dream a little?

He disregards the "Closed for Vacation" sign and opens the front door to the office. The room is washed in sunlight and bright fluorescent overhead light. Deuce steps up to the counter. Normally, fifteen people would be working, but with vacation there are only five. The owner is Sam Levine. He looks up from his desk and gives Deuce a look that's somewhere between condescension and boredom, as if to ask, "Can nobody read the sign?"

"Can I help you?" Levine asks.

Deuce pays him no attention. He puts his valise on the counter and opens it. He pulls a slip of paper from the breast pocket of his suit and studies it. He has the names of some mobbed-up guys whose deposit boxes Ouimette has said not to miss: Jerome Geller, the Bingo Man, Babe Kowal, Mike Ross.

Deuce squints at the piece of paper and, feigning difficulty, tries to softly read the names aloud. Levine grimaces with annoyance and leaves his desk. He walks over to the counter, leans forward to read the note, and Deuce quickly pushes the barrel of his revolver into the little man's nose.

"Touch any alarm button, and I'll blow your head off," Deuce says.

Levine turns white and starts shaking. "You don't know how bad this is, what you are doing," he says.

"Where's the alarm?" Deuce asks softly.

Levine slowly and unsteadily raises an arm and points toward a button midway up the far wall.

"Who else is in the building?"

Levine says there are four other people. His brother Hyman and his sister-in-law Rosalind are at their desks in smaller offices off the corridor. His brother Abraham and the firm's attractive young secretary and apprentice furrier, Barbara Oliva, are about to move a rack of furs through the massive door of the vault.

Deuce orders Sam Levine to call everyone into the office, one at a time. First Hyman, then Rosalind and Abraham. Barbara Oliva hears her name but thinks Sam is mistaken and probably wants only his brother. She turns back to get another rack of furs. Suddenly, Deuce is right beside her.

"Oh, no," Deuce says. "You too."

"Why?" she asks.

Deuce answers with his handgun. He points it straight at her. "Because I said so."

The .38 is only inches from the young woman's face, so she can't help but look straight at it. Without taking her eyes from the revolver, she asks softly, "Are those real bullets in that gun?"

"Are you a fucking comedian?"

Oliva's first thought is that she will not live to see her children again, and that this man with the gun is going to be the reason. She is scared and angry in parts approximately equal. She moves her gaze from the revolver to the man holding it. With only a slight tremor in her voice she says, "I've seen guns before. Get that goddamned thing out of my face."

CHAPTER 26

AT THAT INSTANT, BEFORE DEUCE CAN SAY ANYTHING OR exercise his preference, which would be to slap the pretty blonde across the face, he catches movement on the periphery of his vision. Through the office window he sees Chucky walking quickly toward the building, mask in hand.

Deuce growls at Oliva and, using his gun as a pointer, herds her into the cluster of hostages. Chucky comes through the door struggling with his nylon stocking mask. Oliva notices him and stares straight at him. Chucky moves down the corridor out of sight for an instant then returns, his mask in place and gun in hand.

The two crooks seat their five captives in a semicircle of chairs. Deuce hands out flimsy pillowcases and tells everyone but Sam Levine to put them over their heads. Chucky is looking in every direction at once, taking in the entire office in short darting glances.

The first two-man team should have arrived from the van by now. Two minutes pass. Then another. And another. Deuce and Chucky look at each other. It is the first punch of panic. They wait.

Inside the van, there's mayhem. In fact, there is mutiny. Mitch Lanoue is inching the vehicle along the curb of Cranston Street. The nose of the van is in plain sight from the office window. Deuce and Chucky see it creeping along and realize what's happening. The job is going bad fast. There will be blood. Deuce can see it in Chucky's eyes.

Flynn catches Oliva staring at him. He says to Deuce, "You tell her not to look at me or I'm going to blow her fucking head off."

Oliva needs no prompting. She turns her gaze straight down at the floor. Deuce lowers the gun and adjusts the pillowcase over her head. She is slightly claustrophobic. She gasps and starts to shake. "Please don't make me wear this," she says.

"You have to," Deuce replies.

Outside, Lanoue is a split second from hitting the gas pedal when Joe Danese's anger at the situation rolls through him and blows out like a clap of thunder.

"Crazy Joe" pulls out a hidden snub-nosed .38 and shouts, "Stop. Stop the van. You motherfuckers are going in right now. I'll kill every one of you if you don't fucking move. Get out. Do it. Now!"

The men throw open the doors of the van and tumble onto the pavement, even as the vehicle is stopping. They leave the doors wide open and Lanoue nearly hysterical. He jumps from the van, runs around slamming the doors shut, calling out, "You goddamned sons of bitches, you! Fucking know-nothing assholes. *Sacré bleu!*"

The five men are bogged down with their duffels, a suitcase, an oversize bag, toolboxes, and crowbars. They're stumbling and banging into one another. They all hit the front door at once. They look like the Three Stooges all trying to get through a narrow doorway at the same time. After more swearing and pushing, they manage to get through. They pass the door in single file, each man peering into the office.

Deuce glowers at them; Chucky stares, his eyes like bullets. He's rigid with anger. His arm is extended as straight as a railroad directional aimed at the vault. The masked men look quickly away as they pass.

Deuce turns back to his captives.

"Sam, keep your eyes on the floor," he tells Levine.

Barbara Oliva is weeping softly.

Flynn lifts the hood above her eyes again.

He asks if she's okay.

"I . . . I'm all right," Oliva says.

She looks out into the room again before Deuce lowers the flimsy pillowcase.

Chucky heads for the inner sanctum where the safe deposit boxes are. Minutes later, banging and the sound of electric drills drift out of Bonded Vault.

The biggest heist as of this date in US history finally is under way.

CHAPTER 27

DEUCE LOOKS AT SAM LEVINE AND IS GLAD HE DIDN'T MAKE HIM wear a pillowcase. The old man's color is bad, ranging from gray to white and almost a sickly yellow-green. Deuce needs him free should unexpected business arrive. Now, especially with the rising heat of the morning, Deuce thinks Sam might have died with his head inside a pillowcase. Levine is leaning against the edge of his desk, shaking his head, his eyes fixed on the floor, and he keeps repeating, "You don't know the trouble you bring me." Over and over.

Deuce worries that if he doesn't help him take his mind off the predicament he's in, Sam will either get sick all over the place or have a heart attack. The last thing Deuce wants is for anybody to die on this gig, at least not accidentally. But what to say? What to do? Calm him down, Deuce decides. So he says, "I realize you're upset, Sam, but you know, this is a hell of a way for me to make a living too."

Levine squints at the gunman, terminally perplexed and feeling all the worse for it.

Suddenly the glass front door opens with a bang.

Levine jumps to his feet. The other hostages are startled. Oliva whimpers. Deuce twists toward the door and moves his trigger finger inside the guard of his revolver.

In rushes Lanoue. In a stage whisper that probably can be heard all over the building, he tells Deuce he believes someone has been watching him. The gunman peers out the door and sees a derelict weaving along the sidewalk, straight down the street but more than a block away.

"That son of a bitch couldn't even crawl this far," Deuce shouts. "Goddammit, Harry, get back out there and do your fucking job."

Lanoue turns and leaves. Deuce watches Lanoue through the window as he scrambles toward the van, then he turns back to the hostages. This time the problem is Hyman Levine. He appears to be doing worse than Sam; his breathing is labored. He's sweating profusely.

"Lift your pillowcase up above your nose," the gunman says. "That should help."

Deuce reassures the hostages that everything is okay and will stay that way if they keep doing just as they are told.

"Don't abuse and you won't lose," he tells them calmly.

Then he shrugs, as though embarrassed that he couldn't come up with anything snappier.

CHAPTER 28

AGAIN, DEUCE CATCHES MOVEMENT BEYOND THE WINDOW. HE spots a very old man approaching the front door, a lighted cigarette dangling from his lips. Where the hell is Lanoue this time? Deuce rushes over to greet the visitor as he comes in. The gunman sticks his .38 in the old man's face. "Be quiet and you won't get hurt," Deuce says. The cigarette jiggles a little and there's a puff of smoke, but the man says nothing.

The newcomer has the distinction of being older by far than anyone else in the building. He looks to be somewhere between ninety and a casket. He blinks several times. Smoke drifts from his cigarette. Deuce gently tugs it away from the old guy's mouth, drops the butt on the floor, and grinds it out with his shoe. He guides his guest to a seat beside the other hostages and puts a pillowcase over the old man's head. The latest arrival is Max Gellerman of Warwick, Rhode Island. He is Sam Levine's uncle. Sam Levine doesn't acknowledge Gellerman in any way; Gellerman returns the favor.

A lot of noise is coming from the men deep inside the vault. First it's the high-speed drills and a lot of swearing. The name Harry emanates repeatedly. It is attached to more cursing over and over and over, because the high-speed drilling is going slow. In fact, the men are burning and breaking case-hardened steel drill bits and making no real progress at all.

In frustration, Tarzian jams the flat end of his crowbar behind the edge of the cast-iron collar of the big lock on one of the safe deposit boxes then pulls down hard and quick. Cast iron is strong but brittle. The collar splits in two and falls to the floor with the lock still attached. The door is open. The box inside is pulled to the floor. The sound of its fall is akin to the drop of a manhole cover, and it resonates to shouts of amazement.

There are more men than crowbars, but more than enough internal boxes to be dumped and scoured. One crash follows another. The noise of the locks and then the boxes falling to the floor is broken only by more shouts and hoots and hollers. The men move fast, but they can't stay ahead of the boxes' contents. They do their best to snatch what's most obviously of value. If it is green or glitters, it goes.

Minutes later, Chucky appears at the door to the main office. His mask is perched atop his head and he's steadying himself against the casing. He is drenched in sweat. His eyes are wide and glazed over. His lips, normally thin and tight, betraying no emotion, are curled into a grin so broad and silly it looks like something he borrowed for a Halloween party.

"Harry," he says to Deuce, "you got to see this. It's the fucking jackpot."

Chucky takes Deuce's place while the gunman briefly visits the vault. When Deuce returns to trade places, he's wearing the same silly grin.

The haul is not what John Ouimette promised. It is unbelievably bigger and better. In adventure movies, when pirates finally uncover hidden treasure, the floor of the cave usually is covered in glowing gold and silver coins, jewel-encrusted goblets, sparkling gems, and mounds of jewelry. That's what Deuce and Chucky see. Little wonder they both are dumbstruck.

The heist takes from seventy-five to ninety minutes. The men empty 146 safe deposit boxes. They leave two boxes in the corner unscathed because they didn't have room enough to leverage their crowbars.

"Time to go, Harry," Chucky says. "We got enough"—words Deuce thought nobody would ever hear Chucky say.

CHAPTER 29

Chucky and Danese are the first to leave the building. They are strong men and what any fool would call motivated, and they have all they can do to carry the loot. They hoist it into the van and return for more. Chucky is a little miffed with Danese because, though he did save the day by forcing the nervous crew out of the van and into action, he didn't bring as many satchels and duffels as they could have used, or enough to match the money Chucky gave him. Danese probably gambled it away, Chucky figures.

On the other hand, Chucky says years later, "Who knew there was so much to take?" He has known about the operation for three years, and he has always been certain it would be a good score, but it was not his to make—not without permission. It would be disrespectful, and no doubt suicidal, to act otherwise. He later tells friends that there was so much in those safe deposit boxes, the entire crew could have spent the day trying to empty them, and even then they might not have been able to finish the job.

One of the crew brings out a big green duffle bag crammed with so much loot that he has to drag it. The others who follow do the same. Out of the vault, down the hallway, and out the front door to the sidewalk, where he props it upright against the reopened doors of the van, then bends, lifts, and heaves the bag aboard, sweating and straining.

The dragging and straining and bending and lifting are repeated until all but two of the duffle bags have been muscled aboard. The big van sags under the load. Two remaining satchels go into Byrnes's Chevrolet Monte Carlo.

The van moves off so the loot can be transferred to the other three cars. There are only minutes left now.

The first man into Bonded Vault is the last man out, so it's time for Deuce to wrap things up. He turns to his hostages, tells them he has taken Sam Levine's driver's license so he'll know where to find him if they don't all follow his instructions now.

Deuce was going to just lock everyone in the vault, but Sam Levine said closing the vault door before the programmed end of the business day would trigger the silent alarm, partly a precaution against theft and partly for safety's sake.

Deuce asks his captives if they need to use the bathroom. The pillowcases all nod quickly and in unison.

"Good," he says, "'cause you're all going."

Then he marches his six captives into a tiny toilet stall adjoining the main office. Deuce squeezes everyone inside, shuts the door, and jams a chair under the doorknob.

He leaves the building quickly but not at a run. Byrnes is sitting in his black Monte Carlo at the curb. The car travels only a short distance when Deuce tells Byrnes the car seems to be dogging it. The front of the vehicle is nosed sharply upward, and its rear bumper is only inches off the roadway.

Byrnes looks at him and says, "It's all that weight in the trunk. The silver bars are in there."

"Oh, yeah" Deuce says.

He throws his head back and laughs aloud for the first time all morning.

"The bars of fucking *silver* are in the trunk!" he screams pounding the dashboard. "I hear ya! I hear ya!"

CHAPTER 30

FOR BARBARA OLIVA, THIS IS ONE OF THE WORST MOMENTS of all, as bad as when the pillowcase went over her head. All six people are crunched together and waiting to die inside a funky room the size of an ill-used closet. The room is so small, one person can stand in the middle and touch every wall. For two well-proportioned women to be crushed together against four old men is an indignity in itself.

Oliva never believes that Deuce isn't going to kill them. She fully expects that at any moment, bullets will come tearing through the hollow door and partitioned walls and she will spend her last moments on earth bleeding to death beside a filthy toilet, her blood mingling with the body fluids of five other people, people she works with. They are friends supposedly, but what has been their very first concern? What are they most worried about? What they should report to the police.

"I can't breathe," says one of them.

"Don't talk. You'll use up air."

Silence.

"I don't hear anybody outside."

More silence.

"Kick at the door. Kick at the bottom of the door. Rattle the knob hard."

A few superheated minutes later, the chair that Deuce had wedged under the knob falls to the floor, and the captives fall out into the room.

They go to the cooler and drink all the water they can.

Abraham, Hyman, and Sam start working their way through the mounds of valuables that have been left behind—and there is a lot. The floor of the inner sanctum is covered nearly wall to wall with what the thieves have passed up: mounds and mounds of gold and silver coins; loose, brilliantly colored gems; handguns; gold chalices, some inset with jewels; elegant high-end jewelry, much of it still in individual presentation cases; stock books; and albums of collectors' postage stamps.

They pick up jewelry by the armload and use a shovel to scoop up some of the gold and silver coins scattered all over the inner room of the vault. They stash the valuables in barrels and boxes and push them well out of sight. They grab and empty random containers, stuff valuables in them, and carry them upstairs.

All the while, the brothers are arguing among themselves over what to tell the police and when.

Some people who see the ravaged vault report that apart from the crooks' abandoned tools and bent and broken pry bars, the floor still is literally knee-deep in abandoned treasure by the time police arrive. Others say it is ankle-deep. Barbara Oliva was one of the few to see it.

"It was closer to knee-deep," she says. "What they left behind was so incredible," she said, "it's impossible to imagine what they took."

CHAPTER 31

Minutes tick by, and still the Levines have not called the police. They are dithering, confused, disoriented; more than that, they are quite simply terrified. They do not want to call the police. Their bickering continues. They keep stalling and arguing, and the longer they delay, the angrier Barbara Oliva becomes.

She is already seething for having had a loaded .38 stuck in her face. When she can't take the Levines' dallying and debating any longer, she marches over to the wall of the main office and presses the button that triggers an alarm at Rhode Island Electric Protection Co. In minutes police sirens rise into the thick, superheated haze of the morning and Sam Levine goes silent. His complexion is still grayish white, and he glares at Oliva until the police arrive, but he has no choice but to explain what happened.

He delivers a straightforward account to police. It would have been helpful to know when the safe deposit box operation was set up and who uses it, but Levine doesn't volunteer the information and the police don't ask because, on the face of it, there's nothing illegal going on.

Besides, the police are content to let Levine stew over how he and his brothers, in less than ninety minutes in the heat of a summer morning, have suddenly managed to lose untold valuables carefully entrusted to their safekeeping.

They are quick to notice when Patriarca's shadow passes over his victims. The hint of Mafia action tends to induce amnesia or stupidity among otherwise intelligent people. They forget. They don't hear things. They know nothing. And the Levines are looking like a chorus of those answers.

"Providence police called me the day of the robbery," says Albert E. DeRobbio, then-assistant attorney general, decades after the heist. "And they asked what to do.

"I said, 'Did you do the fingerprinting, talk to the owners and get their statements?'

"They said they did, so I said, 'Well, did you secure the premises?'

"They said they did. So I said, 'I don't think you've got any further obligation in this case,' so they closed it up and left.

"God knows what happened after that. But it was some time before anybody even claimed any losses. I couldn't put it before the grand jury because nobody stepped up to say what had been stolen. Technically, we didn't even really have a robbery."

CHAPTER 32

CHUCKY RETURNS TO THE HIDEOUT FIRST AND PARKS BEHIND the house so no activity will be visible from Golf Avenue. He has a couple of big bags bulging with loot. He jumps from the car and pushes open a bedroom window on the first floor. He tips the bags through the window and climbs through after them. The rest of the crew arrives sporadically. They park out of sight near Chucky and pass the loot to him through the window.

Sometime later, John Ouimette pulls up out front of the house in his jet black Lincoln Continental Mark IV and walks in on bedlam. The treasure is all indoors, and the men are drenched in sweat. The house is hot and airless. Some of the men have stripped to the waist. They are ecstatic but as jumpy as a roomful of ferrets and hurrying sharply, almost without direction. They are hooting and hollering and backslapping and hugging one another.

There is about as much organization to the divvying process as there is honor among thieves. Each of the men tries to keep an eye on the others while daring his own sleight of hand. Gold coins slip away by the handful. Big diamond rings drop into pants pockets. Dazzling, glittering jewels get tucked into ankle socks. Somebody is always checking the windows; all they'd need is for a mail carrier to arrive.

The crooks throw as much of the cash on the twin bed as will fit. All the rest of the loot spills deep across the floor in mounds of gold, necklaces, rings, coins, jewelry boxes, silver, bracelets, and diamond, emerald, and ruby clusters. The volume is extraordinary.

The men begin sorting the cash by throwing matching denominations and marked stacks into big plastic laundry baskets.

Byrnes is sent off to a local market to get two dozen large brown paper bags.

Macaskill uses a calculator to follow the cash count as best he can. He doesn't include armloads of piddling one- and five-dollar bills, just the tens, twenties, fifties, and hundreds. After five thousand dollars is set aside for Walter Ouimette, who stole the vans in addition to chauffeuring Deuce from Boston to East Providence, the tally of cash is $704,000.

That means each of eleven men—Deuce, Chucky, Danese, Byrnes, Tillinghast, Lanoue, Tarzian, Macaskill, John Ouimette, his managing brother Gerard, and their silent patron, Raymond L. S. Patriarca Jr.—should collect sixty-four thousand dollars, not bad for less than ninety minutes of work, at least $873 a minute.

For delivery, the bills are packed tightly in the grocery bags that Byrnes got. The men double the bags for reinforcement. Wouldn't want to drop one in public and have to explain why you're walking around with all of those bundles of dreams.

CHAPTER 33

AROUND NOON, THERE'S A LOUD BANGING ON THE FRONT DOOR of Chucky's hideout. In unison befitting a cartoon, the men dive at the windows. Venetian blinds are snapped shut. Chucky walks slowly to the front door and opens it a crack, holding a revolver behind his back.

A workman is standing on the front steps. "Here to take down the storm windows," the guy says. "Landlord sent us down."

"Yeah," Chucky says. "Okay." Behind him, the entire house exhales. Then the counting resumes, but quietly.

If the same cash robbery were possible today, each of the eleven men would take home nearly $288,000. Little wonder that the folding money had more immediate appeal than the hard glittery stuff. The men stop to admire the sheer grandeur and outrageous heft of fourteen large solid silver ingots, but they're content to bag it up with the rest of the swag and hand it all over to Byrnes and Danese. Byrnes says he will bury it so they can fence it all later.

Nobody gives either the loot or the men in charge of it much more thought. There's no grand plan, no well-orchestrated scheme that will reunite them with the fenced proceeds of their morning's work. Everyone is preoccupied with grabbing his share of cash and putting Rhode Island in the rearview mirror. Danese and Macaskill also take bags for Lanoue and Tarzian, who already have left to dispose of the van.

By early afternoon, only Deuce, Chucky, and Ellen are left in the house. Deuce says good-bye and starts to gather his share. He is about to call a taxi. He's a luxury junkie, and the sooner he's at it the better. "Time to go have some fun with this," he says. "This is what it's all about, right?"

Chucky and Ellen tell him to hold up; he should savor the time. That's their plan, their reason for being. They are in love, after all, and this is the fling of a lifetime. They talk in earnest about their plans. Naturally, they want to get out of town, and they know that as soon as the cops understand how big a job this was, there will be plenty of heat, but who will it come from? They can't exactly complain to their parish pastor now, can they?

For that matter, who are the cops going to look for? Not them. At least at first, everything will point to *Il Padrino*, just because it always does, but the police won't have anything that ties the heist directly to either him or his son, Junior.

Sooner or later, the Old Man will do what he always does: Deny any knowledge, complain that the cops and reporters have been making him a scapegoat for years, insist that he's just an honest businessman, and then tell them all to fuck off. It's his script, all but patented.

Figuring they have a little time, Deuce, Chucky, and Ellen settle on Las Vegas as their destination, and they will go by way of New York City first thing in the morning. Where to stay? The Plaza is nice? Why the hell not?

They check into a suite of rooms and give the bellman a tip he can tell his grandchildren about. After a good night's sleep and a long, leisurely breakfast, the three set out to do some serious shopping. Deuce is very happy. Buy what you want. Money's no object. What could be better? What's life for, if it isn't this?

CHAPTER 34

DEUCE GOES SHOPPING AND BUYS THE MOST EXPENSIVE CLOTHES he can find, not because he needs them but simply because he can. Ellen goes clothes shopping on her own. Chucky goes poking around in jewelry stores.

Two days after the heist, the trio boards a direct flight from New York to Las Vegas. Chucky and Ellen are lovebird happy and seated side by side. Deuce is a short distance away next to some guy who talks from takeoff to landing about what a great place Las Vegas is.

Deuce gleans one important fact from him: The best hotel in the entire city is the MGM Grand. It's right there on The Strip, South Las Vegas Boulevard—that preposterous three-mile mecca of glamour, high-rolling glitz, and neon glow that mobster Bugsy Segal and his friends raised up out of the hot desert sand.

The trio gets in a cab at the airport and Deuce casually tells the driver, "MGM Grand." Chucky and Ellen do a double take in surprise. Deuce just looks at them blankly. "It's the best in Vegas." That's one of the reason's Chucky holds Deuce in such high esteem; he always seems to know these things. It's as though he has access to a part of the world Chucky knows nothing about.

The taxi parks in the MGM Grand's port cochere, and Deuce strides up to the front desk.

"All we have is a suite," the clerk tells him.

"Good. That's just what I want," Deuce says flatly, "a nice suite."

A young bellhop loads their luggage onto a gleaming brass cart and escorts them to a spacious three-room suite. He moves swiftly all around the suite, proudly showing off every accouterment and appurtenance. He says if they need anything, anything at all, just call the front desk and ask for him by name: Ricky Purcell. Deuce tips him one hundred dollars.

Ellen and Chucky have packed thousands of dollars in a valise and don't want to leave it in their hotel room. Deuce volunteers that the hotel has its own safe deposit boxes that guests may use. Chucky is surprised. Deuce is about to take the money downstairs when Chucky takes him aside.

Chucky has a problem. His brow is furrowed, and he looks a little sheepish, which is completely out of character. He says he spent $4,600 of his cash on an engagement ring for Ellen and wants to ask her to marry him, but he wants Deuce's advice on the best way to go about it.

Deuce doubts that Chucky actually bought the ring, but he gives Chucky his best all-knowing smile and says, "I'll take care of it. Give me the ring."

Deuce puts the valise full of cash in a hotel safe deposit box and goes looking for Purcell, who is in the lobby. Clearly it is time for the grand gesture, the kind of suavity that only a would-be high-roller like Deuce could pull off. He gives Purcell the ring, tells him to hook it carefully to the neck of a very good bottle of champagne and bring it up to the suite with one dozen long-stemmed red roses when Ellen returns from shopping. He gives the bellman another couple of hundred dollars for the errand.

Ellen is bowled over. Chucky is happy. He loves Ellen, and he's proud as all hell to have handled the proposal with flair; it's one more reason he and Deuce are so close: Deuce always knows such good stuff.

CHAPTER 35

WITH THE TWO LOVEBIRDS ACCOUNTED FOR, DEUCE SET HIS sights on finding a woman of his own. He isn't about to waste time wining and dining. This is Las Vegas, after all. You want the company of a woman, you buy it.

He picks a likely candidate from one of the continuously updated catalogs that are everywhere in the hotels. He calls the phone number listed for an attractive young brunette and, sure enough, in less time than it takes to invent a story about who he is and what he's doing in town, not that anyone would care, he's got himself a three-hundred-dollar woman.

She is as pretty as advertised, but she no sooner comes to the door than another woman shows up, a friend of a croupier Deuce had spoken with earlier. He had asked the guy if he personally could recommend a sweet young thing. He said he could, but Deuce didn't expect action this fast.

The croupier's friend, actually his prostitute wife's friend, is a knockout. She is younger than the girl from the catalog, in her early twenties, five feet two inches tall and slender. She's well built, with big green eyes and a melt-your-heart smile, and she says her name is Karyne Sponheim.

Deuce says his name is Dennis Allen. He is dazzled. With the other woman in the room behind him, he explains his situation, peels three hundred-dollar bills from a roll in his pocket, and hands them to Karyne, who smiles and leaves.

The next day she is still a vivid memory, so Deuce sends Purcell to find her, which he does. Karyne is no unplucked flower blossom. She is a hooker, but she hasn't been at it long enough to look hard or jaded; quite the opposite. She's bubbly, intensely and eternally interested in whatever Deuce has to say, and she is as enthusiastic about sex as he is. The gunman from Lowell has found his heart's desire.

Karyne falls for Deuce about as hard and fast as he falls for her. The pay-as-you-go sex ends nearly as fast as it starts. The two quickly become inseparable, and so Deuce and Karyne and Chucky and Ellen settle down to wring all the fun they can out of the one city in America with the loudest, brassiest boast that its specialty is fun of any and every kind.

CHAPTER 36

In the capital cities of many states, the exposure and ransacking of a secret Mafia depository might be something of an embarrassment; not so in Providence, at least not in any terribly obvious way. Mayor Vincent A. "Buddy" Cianci Jr. downplays it, as any chief executive would. He points out that despite all the talk of goods worth millions being stolen, no one actually has claimed extraordinary losses. He's right of course, but his naysaying is just damage control. The truth is, he is angry. Cianci is a proud man and proudly Italian. He sees *La Cosa Nostra* as a blight, and he campaigned on an anticrime pledge. Worst of all, a caper of Bonded Vault's magnitude is not soon forgotten, and that tarnishes the city he loves.

The FBI gets involved in the investigation early. Figuring that goods this glittery are too hot to fence quickly in this country, agents try tracing the stolen jewelry through a team of contacts in Bern, Switzerland, and Bonn, Germany, but get nowhere. This is unfortunate, because the two police commands that will have to unravel the brazen robbery, the Rhode Island State Police and the Providence Police Department, do not have a history of cooperating with each other.

The state police are run by Superintendent Col. Walter E. Stone, an uncompromising law enforcement legend, one of several high-ranking and widely respected cops who first testified in Congress to the existence of organized crime in America.

Stone's troopers are carefully selected, bright, well paid, highly trained, blade-straight, by the book, and paramilitary. They wear jodhpur uniforms of slate gray whipcord with red piping and trim black ties; Sam Browne belts; three-quarter-length coats; wide, flat-brimmed Stetsons; and lace-up, knee-high brown leather boots. They drive big-mill Ford Interceptor LTDs the color of burnished silver, and they do not routinely trust cops from lesser Rhode Island departments, which is to say, all thirty-eight of them.

Providence police, under the blustering but savvy control of lame-duck Col. Walter A. McQueeney, appear lackluster by comparison, but not for lack of some tough, hard-working and intelligent cops. They just don't like the state police.

Providence cops wear standard-issue chocolate brown uniforms with matching caps, the same design as those worn by most every other cop in the land. They joke that it takes the average Rhode Island State Police trooper three hours to get dressed, and they routinely dismiss them as peacocks, glory hounds, and AAA with a badge.

Cianci, looking back over forty years, still smiles. "Cops are just trying to climb the ladder like everyone else, and there's always a lot of angling and jealousy in the ranks. So, yeah, when the state police are involved it can be a problem. But from about the level of captain on up, where the bigger cases are handled, look out. They'll do anything and everything they can to get a good collar, even if it means cooperating."

From the beginning, the police labor with the presumption that no heist as big as the Bonded Vault job goes down without someone somewhere knowing something about it, so first comes the sorting, grinding and sifting—the routine procedural work, statements from witnesses, reviews, re-interviews, follow-ups, interview comparisons, team briefings, and consultations behind closed doors. And then detectives turn to their most reliable weapons: rats and snitches, the little guys, the hangers-on who suck up to the bigger guys, the ones who ingratiate themselves to even bigger guys, who throw them crumbs for jobs and whose livelihoods

Walpole State Prison photos of Robert "Deuce" Dussault; 1974 and 1968. MASS. DEPT. OF CORRECTIONS

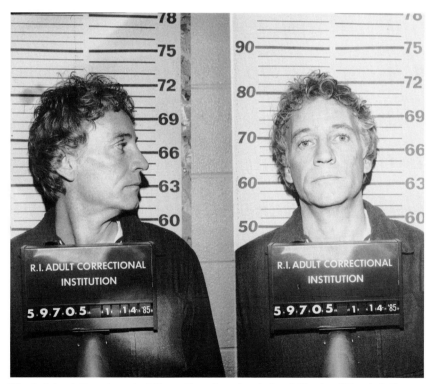

Rhode Island Department of Corrections inmate photo of Charles "Chucky" Flynn, 1976. RI DEPT. OF CORRECTIONS

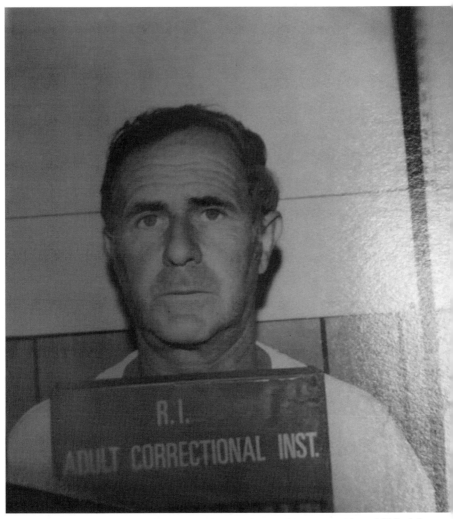

Rhode Island Department of Corrections inmate photo of Lawrence Marcel "Mitch" Lanoue, 1978. RI DEPT. OF CORRECTIONS

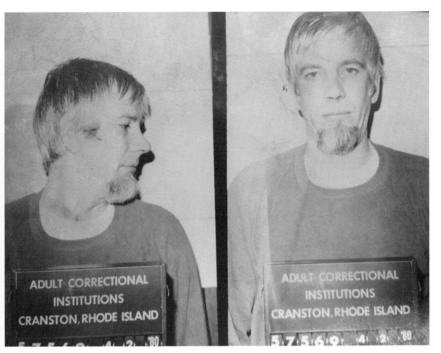

Rhode Island Department of Corrections inmate photo of Robert "Mac" Macaskill, 1980. RI DEPT. OF CORRECTIONS

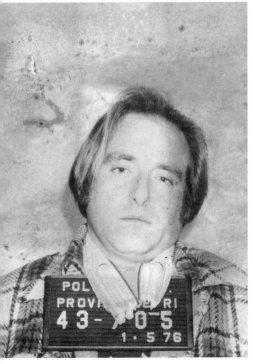

Providence Police booking photo of Ralph "Skippy" Byrnes, 1976. PROVIDENCE POLICE

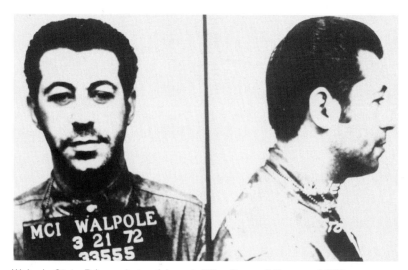

Walpole State Prison photo of Joseph "The Dancer" Danese, 1972.
MASS. DEPT. OF CORRECTIONS

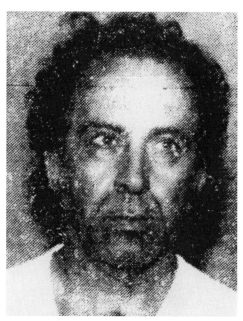

Undated police booking photo of Jacob
"The Snake" Tarzian. UNKNOWN

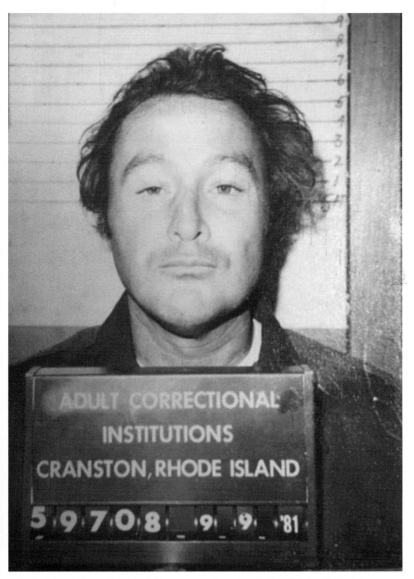

Rhode Island Department of Corrections inmate photo of John Ouimette, 1981. RI DEPT. OF CORRECTIONS

Raymond L.S. Patriarca outside Providence Superior Court in 1963.
PHOTO CREDIT: THE *PROVIDENCE JOURNAL*

The Hudson Fur Storage and Bonded Vault building located at 101 Cranston St., 2015.
PHOTO CREDIT: JOHN VILLELLA

Karyne Sponheim and Robert "Deuce" Dussault in Las Vegas, 1975.

Robert "Deuce" Dussault while being held at the R.I. State Police headquarters, 1977. PHOTO COURTESY: THE *PROVIDENCE JOURNAL*

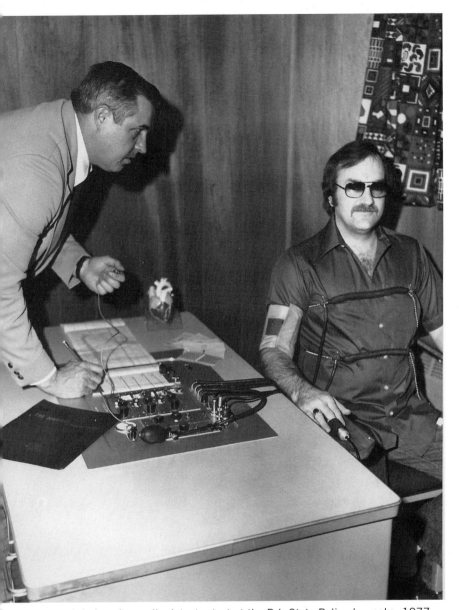

Robert Dussault being given a lie detector test at the R.I. State Police barracks, 1977.

Robert Dussault and author Randall Richard at the R.I. State Police Barracks, 1977.
PHOTO COURTESY: THE *PROVIDENCE JOURNAL*

The late investigative Reporter Jack White (front, left), Robert Dussault (front, center), author Randall Richard (front, right), State Police Detective Michael Urso (back, left), attorney John Toscano (back, right), 1977. PHOTO COURTESY: THE *PROVIDENCE JOURNAL*

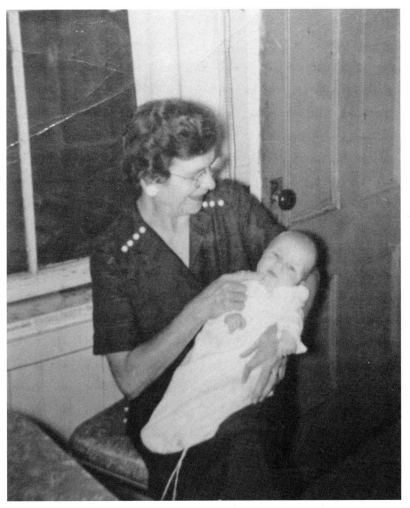

Undated photo of Elizabeth Dussault holding Robert Dussault as an infant in Lowell, Massachusetts. PHOTO COURTESY: THE DUSSAULT FAMILY

Undated Dussault family photo taken in Lowell, Massachusetts. Robert Dussault is in the back, center. PHOTO COURTESY: THE DUSSAULT FAMILY

uthor Tim White inside Bonded Vault in Providence, 2010.
PHOTO BY: JOHN VILLELLA/WPRI-TV

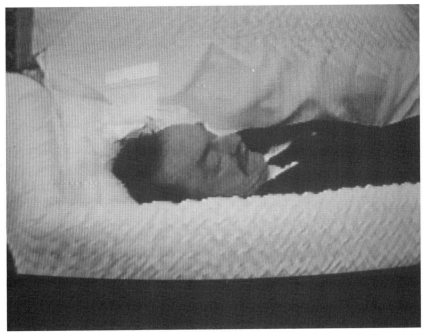

Still image from video taken of Robert Dussault's aka Robert Dempsey's funeral in
Minot, North Dakota, 1992. PHOTO COURTESY: WPRI-TV

Still image from WPRI-TV news footage the day of the Bonded Vault Heist, Aug. 14, 1975
PHOTO COURTESY: WPRI-TV

Authors Randall Richard (left) and Wayne Worcester (right) in Lowell, Massachusetts.
PHOTO BY: TIM WHITE

depend on knowing the streets and who is calling which shots when, where, and why.

The trick is to convince the guy that it's in his best interest to tell what he knows. Sounds simple. In fact, it is leagues away from that. It is not the kind of thing anyone just sits down one day to do. It's what good detectives accomplish very gradually over a long period of time, learning who is important to whom and under what circumstances, steadily building small networks of well-placed informers, manipulating systems of rewards, favors, and blind spots, some little, some not so little, but all geared to developing the pressure it takes to make the rat release critical information when it is needed the most.

What matters most is that all of the pressure is brought to bear on the right man. In a very real sense, the guy with the best rat wins.

CHAPTER 37

THE DAY AFTER THE ROBBERY, SAM LEVINE PETITIONS THE superior court to put Bonded Vault in receivership, thereby relinquishing responsibility for any of the valuables the robbers left behind. The fate of what remains is put in the hands of Thomas R. DiLuglio of Johnston, a tough lawyer who two years hence will become the lieutenant governor of Rhode Island.

This amounts to the Levines saying, "You've got a problem with what you had in those boxes? You take it up with him."

The list of box holders is leaked to the press. The effect is a lot like turning over a rock and watching all the little critters scurry in search of new darkness in which to prosper. At least one in every five names has a recognizable link to organized crime, and the likelihood is that a good many of the other names are merely fakes or shells on loan from friends or relatives.

The Internal Revenue Service quickly puts a lien on all the "unidentifiable and unclaimed" valuables the robbers left behind and asks the court to freeze all the company's assets until it can be determined how they should be distributed.

The IRS is looking for assets belonging to a host of box holders in whom the government has a special interest:

William A. and Mildred A. Lamphere of Cranston, a coin dealer and his wife, who the agency asserts owes the government nearly $691,000 in back taxes.

Frank "Babe" Kowal, under indictment for possession of stolen goods, has access to four boxes under an assumed name.

one point he throws the dice for twenty-four hours straight, and they are cold all the way; he couldn't warm them up if he set fire to his bankroll. He borrows some money from Deuce so he can keep playing.

Ellen is distraught. She tells Deuce in a teary-eyed, frustrated rush that Chucky has even gone through the stacks of five-hundred-dollar bills that he had. She might as well have dumped a bucket of ice water over Deuce's head. He is stunned, not so much by news of the loss, but because he had no idea that Chucky, whose highest professed ideal always has been loyalty, apparently cut everybody, including his best friend, out of what had to have been a lot of additional cash from the heist—tens of thousands of dollars more at least. Deuce figures Chucky must have set it aside right after the robbery, before everyone got back to the hideout. It's not that Deuce might not have done the same thing if he'd had the chance; he is a thief, after all. It's just that this secret little sleight of hand somehow feels sort of personal; it hurts, but he shakes it off.

Ellen is frantic over Chucky's losses, and she says she wants to go home; they argue. He goes back to the craps tables. Deuce follows him, watches him lose more money, talks him into taking a break, and then convinces him that Ellen is right. Chucky's on a losing streak that can't be broken. Next day, the couple flies home.

CHAPTER 39

LAS VEGAS CAN WEAR DOWN THE MOST DEVOTED OF REVELERS after a while, so Deuce arranges for Purcell to take him and Karyne on a sightseeing tour of California. Karyne is disappointed. She knows California well and is eager to show Deuce all there is to see. "Why didn't you ask me?" So he does. Purcell stays in Las Vegas, and Deuce and Karyne go to San Francisco and take in the sights for several days. Then they drive—Karyne always behind the wheel—leisurely down through Big Sur and along the spectacular California coast. They head toward Los Angeles, tour Hollywood and stop when they reach Beverly Hills. Where to stay? The famed Beverly Hills Hotel, of course.

Deuce's eyes light up when he sees the lobby. There is a boutique on one side, a small jewelry store on the other. He figures the window jewelry alone is good for five million dollars, and the place is run by just one person. Despite his best instincts, he rents a room, and he and Karyne get comfortable in a cabana by the pool.

He spots David Hartman, host of ABC's *Good Morning America*, and quite by accident ends up being introduced to famed author Harold Robbins and a few retired actresses. So many famous people are paged almost one after another that Deuce starts to feel as though his head is on a swivel looking for celebrities.

Deuce and Karyne are tourists too. They pop into a few shops on Rodeo Drive for some baubles, take day trips to Disneyland, and do some gambling at a racetrack outside of San Diego.

Partly out of his warped sixth sense and partly out of plain old curiosity, Deuce calls a guy near Rhode Island who knows him by one of the several aliases he contrived over the years and asks what's going on.

Deuce tells him he's out in California vacationing but figures he'll be back pretty soon. He likes the fall, the changing leaves and all, even when he's looking at them through steel bars, because he knows Christmas is coming. He feels it in his bones. It's only September, but his homing instinct is keen.

His friend tells him that about a month ago there was this big robbery at some fur storage place in Providence that turned out to have tons of loot nobody knew about. He says it's been all over the papers and even on TV. The word is millions of bucks walked out of the place. Some of Raymond's guys probably. It's odd though. The cops are after some guy named Dussault. You'd have thought they'd be hunting an Italian.

CHAPTER 40

DEUCE ISN'T EXACTLY SHOCKED THAT HE IS WANTED BY THE police, but he is surprised that he has been identified so quickly. Jail is always a prospect. When he pulls a job, he never wears a disguise or a mask, partly because they are always a pain in the neck and can get in your way, and partly because they seem stupid. Somebody sees you going into a jewelry store wearing a mask, it's a safe bet they'll get a quick grasp of the situation. As for identifying him, well, eyewitness accounts and descriptions are notoriously unreliable; any cop will tell you that. So Deuce just goes in fast and hard, orders people not to look at him, and hopes for the best. Half the time, it works pretty well; on the other hand, half is just about as much of his life as he has spent in jail.

Still, he is saddened a bit. The past few weeks have been the time of his life, and he'd just as soon see this run with Karyne stretch a good distance into the future. He goes back to the cabana in a more somber mood but does his best to hide it from his girlfriend, which works for a while. But over the next couple of days, he starts drinking more than usual, which is a lot, and that darkens his mood. He and Karyne argue over some minor thing; he explodes in anger, grabs her by the neck, and throws her across the bed, calling her a miserable little cunt and other obscene and unkind things too numerous to mention. This isn't the Dennis she knows; it's somebody else, and she is afraid of him.

Deuce packs his bags. Karyne is distraught and in tears. Dennis is about to leave her over what? Some stupid little argument? It makes no sense. When she says so, Deuce only gets angrier and calls her more obscene names. He calls Purcell and hires him to drive him to Los Angeles International Airport. Deuce is going back to Rhode Island. It'll be like hiding the pearl in a fishbowl, a plain-sight place no one will think to look. He'll find Chucky; they'll figure out what to do.

By the time the silver Lincoln pulls into the airport, Deuce has calmed down a bit, thought things over. He bought the car for Chucky. How's he going to get it to him? And what about all of the stuff he bought? He takes a deep breath, goes to a telephone, and calls Karyne, who is still in the hotel room sobbing. He apologizes until he runs out of appropriate words. She agrees to pack up the rest of their bags and meet him in a lounge at the airport.

When they meet, he apologizes again, tells her what he does for a living, and that the police back East are looking for him. His voice jitters when he says everything just fell in on him all of a sudden and that's why he blew up at her. Karyne by now is composed and relatively unfazed; no schoolgirl she. He's still her Denny, and they are still a couple. Karyne says, in fact, that she loves Deuce; he says he loves her too.

CHAPTER 41

DEUCE BUYS PURCELL A RIDE BACK TO LAS VEGAS, AND HE AND Karen head east, this time as fugitive tourists. They visit the Grand Canyon, Old Faithful at Yellowstone National Park, then Mount Rushmore and the Badlands of South Dakota, all the more majestic from the front seat of a convertible. Deuce calls Chucky several times, partly because more than ever now he wants to know what's going on, and partly because his money is running out and he'd like some more of what he's certain was a job that netted more than his sixty-four-thousand-dollar share.

Deuce says he wants another hundred thousand dollars. Chucky says he'll see what he can do, but it's clear something is amiss. Chucky sounds cautious and, in fact, a little stiff, almost wary, but he agrees to meet Deuce at a motel at O'Hare International Airport in Chicago.

Two days later, Chucky checks into a room at the hotel. Karyne waits in the hotel lounge while Deuce goes up to Flynn's room. Chucky is there. So is Skippy Byrnes.

Deuce barely acknowledges Byrnes and gets quickly to the point. Did Chucky bring him the money? Flynn hands over about $8,500. He says the guys took up a collection for him, and now they're trying to fence the Bonded Vault loot in one big deal; that's likely to take some time.

Deuce says nothing. The silence is uncomfortable.

"Did you leave any fingerprints behind?" Chucky asks.

"What? Nah," Deuce says, "you know me better than that."

"Well," Chucky says, "that thing that you touched . . ."

During the robbery, Deuce asked Sam Levine if he had an office cash box. Levine said he did. Deuce said, let's have it. The gray steel box contained petty cash, a couple of hundred dollars, no more. Deuce took it, and all the while was careful to handle the box only by its edges.

"Remember I had to wipe that thing 'cause you left prints all over it?" Chucky says.

Deuce is irked. "Hey, wait a minute. You know me better than that. I didn't leave no fingerprints behind there. What the hell's the story? What's happening?"

"The cops say they got your prints."

"That's bullshit and you know it, Chucky. They're making that up because somebody must have fingered me, and they're covering for him. Some son of a bitch ratted me out."

CHAPTER 42

THE POLICEMEN WHO TACKLE THE BONDED VAULT CASE ARE the sort others are inclined to describe as "cops' cops." These guys are rarely off the mark. They can be controversial or occasionally brash. Mostly they are unflinchingly tough, bright, thorough, and downright ruthless in pursuit of those who are incorrigibly and determinedly their opposite.

Each of them works several cases, so they rotate in and out of the heist investigation, but Bonded Vault is a priority.

The highest-ranking officer is State Police Maj. Lionel "Pete" Benjamin, Col. Walter Stone's hand-picked number-two man and chief of detectives. He is ramrod straight, five feet nine inches tall, weighs in at about 190 pounds, and has a barrel for a chest. His hair is dark, thinning, combed straight back, and his smile is so perfectly white that it's disarming. Benjamin is the impeccable embodiment of what Stone wants every one of his troopers to be, and he is the most cunning of men.

No matter which side of the law you're on, every promise, every kindness, every wrong or slippery deed, whether done for a greater good or a lesser evil, has a consequence. It's Newton's third law, and heroes and villains alike are suckled on it: For every action, there is an equal and opposite reaction. Sometimes you can predict it, sometimes you can't, which is precisely what makes the playing of the game fundamentally nasty and inherently dangerous.

It falls to Benjamin to help Stone develop a network of informants who can pry open a private window on organized crime. It's no small chore, working snitches. Give a little, get a little, and always put it to work. Bit by bit by hard-won bit, the commerce of detection is always in progress—whispered tips, secrets, requests, and favors; innumerable dances with the devil and all of his wretched, cloven-hooved friends.

Stone and Benjamin years ago set up an Organized Crime Intelligence Unit within the state police.

One of its mainstays is Det. Lt. Vincent Vespia Jr. He knows *Il Padrino* and a good many of his associates because he grew up with many of them on Federal Hill. Vespia is handsome, quick, and unafraid. He once donned a football helmet and shoulder pads and, carrying a shotgun, raided an illegal gambling enterprise on the Hill by crashing through a second-floor window from the raised basket of a cherry picker.

There's Lt. Michael Urso, soft-spoken, built like a defensive lineman, and instrumental in some of the state's biggest cases.

Another is Lt. Anthony J. Mancuso, a well-liked, savvy, and particularly resourceful investigator.

Immediately after the robbery, they turn up the heat on their cluster of confidential informants, and Benjamin presses one man in particular, one of the best-placed, longest lived, and most reliable rats anywhere in the Northeast—a cruel and cold-blooded, red-headed killer named Richard Gomes of North Providence, Rhode Island, aka "Red Bird."

CHAPTER 43

FOR HIS ENTIRE EXECRABLE LIFE, PRISON HAS BEEN A REVOLVING
door for Richard Gomes. Forget the arrests and reform school
sentences for breaking and entering. Start at about age eighteen
with a five-year sentence for desertion as his army unit is about to
be sent into combat in Korea. Follow that with a court martial and
another sentence to forty-five years of hard labor in Fort Leav-
enworth, Kansas, for rioting that nearly destroys his jail at Camp
Gordon, Georgia.

After several years and amnesty, return home to Rhode Island.
Then stab a guy to death in the basement of a bar, get caught with
seven kilos of hashish, get pinched again with some serious weight
of cocaine, help two other mugs beat a guy nearly to death with
lead pipes, pump four rounds into two guys minding their own
business sitting in their car eating wieners, playing music that to
your way of thinking is too loud, and, well, one prison or another
is bound to become your mailing address.

In the late 1960s Gomes is serving time in the federal pen-
itentiary in Lewisburg, Pennsylvania, when he becomes a close
friend and confidant of one John Gotti, the infamous "Dapper
Don," crime boss of New York's notorious Gambino *La Cosa Nostra* family. When they get out, the man with the kinky, unruly red
hair nicknamed Red Bird becomes a personal driver for Gotti.

In the 1970s Gomes is able to move as smoothly as a serpent
between the Gambino and Patriarca families, usually, though not
exclusively, by way of Gerard Ouimette and the Frenchman's long-
suffering renegade mobsters. He is one more conduit between the

families and their myriad associates, and that makes him a most valuable resource—to mobsters, for the work he does, and to the police, who need to keep his role as informer buried as deeply as possible. With the exception of seven weeks' earned-release time for Red Bird—July 16 to August 27, the same span in which Bonded Vault is pulled off—he and Ouimette are imprisoned and running Steel City.

The public drives by Rhode Island's state prison and sees a medieval creation, a threatening complex of thick, dark, towering granite walls, crenellated and topped with razor wire, something straight out of an old prison movie, and presumes serious criminal activity therein is impossible. In fact, there are messengers who make it easy for thugs like Ouimette to manage their gangs almost as if they were with them on the street. And when the work proves taxing, they occasionally manage to get some of their meals catered.

Inside with Red Bird and Ouimette as of August 27, and certainly not for the first time, is another career heavy, Ralph DiMasi, who spent some of his formative years as a thug in Lowell before moving to Rhode Island.

Court records, according to a story in the *Providence Journal*, show that some years ago, when DiMasi was in prison and especially vexed by a particular judge, he wrote him a nasty note on toilet paper, telling the judge, in quite impressive penmanship, that when he was through reading the missive, he could shove it up his ass.

CHAPTER 44

DiMasi is stunned by news of the Bonded Vault robbery and can't help but marvel at whoever had the guts to pull it off. When he finds out that the bandits are guys he has known for years and even pulled jobs with, he is blind angry they didn't cut him in; this makes him ripe for use as a rat.

Of course for that to matter, the rat catchers have to suspect that DiMasi or one of his cronies could be a player in this underbelly drama. As it happens, just such men are watching, listening, and waiting: the acting chief of Providence police detectives, for one.

Pasquale "Pat" Rocchio grew up in Silver Lake, joined the Marines after high school, and has been with the department since 1955, when he became a beat cop on Raymond's Federal Hill. He's an open, friendly guy with a quick smile. Rocchio is one of Chief McQueeney's favorites, and for good reason. In fifteen years as a beat cop, Rocchio closes a lot of cases, and as he moves through the ranks, he becomes one of the department's all-time most decorated men—about two dozen commendations by 1975.

Working with them all is Sgt. William B. "Billy" Giblin, another decorated veteran. Giblin is almost as controversial a cop as the department has. He earned his rank on the beat. He is Irish tough and sharp, a street-legal knuckle-buster with a look that says he has seen it all twice and didn't like it much the first time.

The police are working their sources hard, and they're doing it together.

Progress comes fast.

Dussault wore no mask, so there is no shortage of witnesses to describe his features for the department's sketch artist.

Within eight days of the robbery, by August 22, Gomes has given the state police, through Benjamin, a name to go with the picture. The FBI's Boston office notifies headquarters in Washington, DC, that Deuce is the prime suspect in the heist.

Separately, the Providence police detectives are shaking down their own sources, and DiMasi, who is charged with possession of burglary tools and a firearm, receiving stolen goods, assault with a deadly weapon, assault with intent to murder, and conspiracy to murder, suddenly is happy to offer Rocchio and Giblin a name that might earn some leniency.

Try Bobby Dussault, he says.

That's Deuce times three, counting the sketch, and three of a kind is easily enough for Assistant Attorney General DeRobbio to win the hand, because Matthew Levine, the youngest of his clan, finally fesses up to using one of Bonded Vault's safe deposit boxes to hide at least one hundred thousand dollars.

His admission of loss means DeRobbio finally has a reluctant victim, an incident that meets the law's full and formal definition of an armed robbery for which someone can be prosecuted. And now he has a candidate—a career criminal who has been vetted by two of the best-placed informants in New England, culled independently from two of the state's top law enforcement agencies. DeRobbio's information is solid. On August 29, Attorney General Julius C. Michaelson convenes a grand jury to hear evidence in the case; six days later, on September 3, the panel hands down a twenty-count indictment charging Deuce for the armed robbery of Bonded Vault.

The indictment reads like the menu at an all-you-can-eat crook's buffet: one count of entering a building in the daytime with intent to rob, five counts of robbery, four counts of kidnapping, five counts of assault with a dangerous weapon, possession of a firearm, possession of a firearm while committing a crime of violence, possession of a firearm after a previous conviction of a crime of violence, and possession of burglary tools.

Figuring the gunman isn't dumb enough to still be in Rhode Island, Michaelson files a warrant with the US attorney's office for Deuce's arrest on a charge of unlawful flight to avoid prosecution.

The charges probably would have been the same even if Deuce had used a loaded gun during the heist. He thought he was, but he never checked. Chucky removed the live ammunition and replaced it with blank cartridges before he gave the gun to him.

There was nothing wrong with the gun. It was a perfectly good weapon, a snub-nose Smith & Wesson Model 15-3, and it certainly would have fired. A guy in Warwick, Rhode Island, had bought it on January 26, 1971, from Jimmy's Gun Store on Union Avenue in Cranston, Rhode Island, and kept it where no one ever would have thought to look, under the mattress in his bedroom. So when some bum broke into the house on March 14, 1974, the gun, as they say, went missing, along with a police scanner and the guy's coin collection.

While Deuce dislikes using a gun, he does concede that they are a distinct asset when you're robbing someone. The problem is, Deuce can't always be trusted with bullets, and Chucky thinks this is one of those times. All of Deuce's complaints about the crew, his constant bitching about working for the Italians, his swaggering insistence that he is somehow above the other guys—all of it has finally gotten to Chucky. John Ouimette told him that he and Raymond Patriarca Jr. conceived the heist, *Il Padrino* okayed it, and they were leaving it to him to carry it out. This is no small errand. In fact, Chucky considers the heist a privilege. He has known of the vault's existence for at least three years because he knows some of the crooks who come and go from the place.

Chucky picked Deuce to lead the actual robbery, and Deuce should have been grateful for the chance. Instead, all he did was piss and moan about it right up to the last minute. Chucky would be held accountable if it all went sideways, not Deuce, so he wasn't about to take any chances.

Chucky loves Deuce, but old friend or not, the son of a bitch is off his game. He was sheepish about taking a role in the attempt to kill Rudy Sciarra, so Chucky gave him a sawed-off shotgun to carry just so Deuce could save face with the crew; only Deuce and Chucky knew the sawed-off wasn't loaded; Chucky kept the shells in his pocket. But then came the coin shop robbery that Deuce was supposed to run. Instead, he let it turn into a joke. It was Lanoue who messed up, but the job was Deuce's responsibility.

If the big heist were to turn bad and Deuce had a loaded gun in his hand, who knows what might happen? If one of the hostages tried to be a hero and needed killing, he couldn't count on Deuce to do it. Chucky wouldn't flinch. Besides, he had his own secret backup: Joe Danese was always armed for a job.

Deuce's indictment so soon after the heist takes everyone in Ouimette's gang by surprise, especially Chucky. He looks at that fabled old writing on the wall, sees it slipping down to the floor he's standing on, and is not quite certain what to make of it; nothing good, that's for sure.

CHAPTER 45

WERE YOU TO TAKE A BLANK MAP OF THE UNITED STATES AND plot Deuce and Karyne's whereabouts on it for most of the fall, you'd end up with something akin to a Jackson Pollock painting. Connect the dots and slashes and splotches and splashes and lines and what they reveal is . . . well, nothing beyond the beholder's eye. There is a compelling and dark kind of depth there but no pattern, no route to be duplicated, nothing to be followed, and certainly no one to be beheld, which of course is why the lovebirds keep moving.

Fall is flirting with winter now, and outlaw life is getting old. The novelty of touring and sightseeing and moving from hotel to motel to motor court is wearing off, no matter where they are. When they stop anywhere for more than a couple of days, the air gets thinner, the barometer drops, and they feel the pressure that comes from living life in snatches. No need to talk about it. They're fugitives. They know that no matter where they are or when, or what they may appear to be doing, they're running.

The little fissures and cracks in their relationship open up. They are quicker to disagree, more likely to argue and drink heavily, and when they do, Deuce knocks Karyne around some more. They make up, reinvent sex, find a way to pretend this spat is the last one, and then they hit the road again.

They've also taken to popping black beauties, amphetamines, here and there, partly for a sense of euphoria and partly just so they can stay awake for long stretches on the road. They may be at Karyne's small apartment just off The Strip in Las Vegas one week. The next they're in Dallas or Houston, maybe Minneapolis, or Boston. Periodically, Deuce calls Chucky and asks for more money.

Chucky meets them a second time in Chicago and gives Deuce another thousand dollars, bringing Deuce's total welfare bonus from Chucky to $9,500. Chucky says he is fed up with being pestered for more money, even if it's Deuce who needs it. Chucky says he's stopping the cash flow until there's some return from the fence who's supposed to be handling the Bonded Vault loot. Deuce says he understands. He and Karyne tell Chucky they're off to Dallas, get in her little Dodge compact, and head southwest for Dallas, leaving the luxurious new Lincoln convertible with Chucky.

Karyne is doing nearly all the driving, but sometimes if the day is bright and they're in a part of the Midwest where the sky goes all the way down to the ground and there is nothing but open road in front of them, Deuce takes the wheel. He likes driving for a while, but only if the road is straighter than he is. Karyne's Dodge compact is not an automatic, and Deuce is slow to get the hang of shifting. This leaves Karyne to chauffer them for mile upon countless mile.

Less than a week later, the odyssey turns bitter. What does it is a story in the November 2 *Providence Sunday Journal* involving Deuce, an unidentified middleman, and a small-time lawyer later identified as Robert J. Kelly from Attleboro, Massachusetts, just over the Rhode Island line. On an average map, the city is only about a quarter of an inch northeast of Providence. The story comes much closer than that to causing an explosion.

CHAPTER 46

THE LAWYER SAYS HE IS REPRESENTING AN INTERMEDIARY FOR Deuce, who promises he will turn himself over to the police if they will guarantee him immunity from prosecution and a new identity in exchange for his cooperation.

Kelly says the middleman also wants the deal to include one hundred thousand dollars: fifty thousand for Deuce, twenty-five thousand for Deuce's girlfriend, and twenty-five thousand for himself.

Kelly says the intermediary, whom he refuses to identify, has met twice with police since the heist, but he personally attended only one session. He says he was left with the distinct impression that negotiation was possible: Deuce and the police who have been searching for him for more than ten weeks, may cut a deal.

Neither Stone, for the state police, nor McQueeney, for the Providence police, will confirm the report.

Regardless of anything the lawyer says, Stone is as implacable as his name suggests. McQueeney is apoplectic. He would curtsy before the queen of England sooner than he'd be party to such a negotiation.

McQueeney also goes out of his way to insist that the worth of the loot from the heist may only be $105,000, because that's the most recent total of financial loss that box holders have claimed—a far, far cry from the three-million-dollar figure reporters are now using. McQueeney demands that the reporters disclose their sources of information.

Mayor Buddy Cianci stands with the chief on the issue of financial loss, but his support ends there. He has been mayor for less than a year, and the robbery already has drawn far more widespread attention to the city's underbelly than he cares for. "No one wants this thing blown out of proportion," Cianci says.

But McQueeney persists. He asks Michaelson to convene a grand jury in order to subpoena the reporters. Instead the attorney general asks the reporters to meet him in his office for a discussion and says they should bring their notes with them. The reporters refuse; in the end, Michaelson concludes that they have that right.

John Ouimette's response to the story is quicker and considerably different. He tells Chucky to pick up Joe Danese and Skippy Byrnes, find Deuce, and kill him.

CHAPTER 47

FIVE DAYS LATER, ON NOVEMBER 7, KARYNE AND DEUCE ARE dozing in their plush suite at the Hilton Hotel in Dallas when the telephone rings. Deuce picks up. The voice he hears is Chucky's. The flatness of it is familiar, but the tone is wrong; if you tried to wring a warm, friendly sound from a cold, suffering thing, you'd have it. Deuce hears blood in Chucky's voice. He gets to his feet, swallowing hard, stretching the phone cord as he reaches for his suitcase and starts throwing clothing in it.

" . . . You're my best friend," Chucky says, "and you know I've never hurt you. Is that broad with you? Well, do me a favor and don't tell her nothing. . . . Don't tell her it's me talking to you, and you just stay there and we'll be right out. We're flying right out. We've got to talk to you, you know? . . . You sure you'll be there? . . . You're my friend. You aren't going to make me go out there for nothing, right?"

Subtlety is not Chucky's long suit. In the end, the mob always uses someone close to you; Deuce knows that and sees his immediate future with an awful clarity. He does his best to keep his own voice under control, but as soon as he puts the phone down, he shakes Karyne awake and tells her, "We're leaving. We're going to Vegas." By then he is almost packed.

Karyne is groggy, annoyed at being rousted. Deuce is still stuffing clothes into his suitcase. "Look," he says, "there's an article in the Providence paper, and some friends are coming down to kill me. If they come in here and you're here, they'll kill you too. They don't give a damn!"

Karyne is up, shuffling across the floor, muttering about friends who are willing to kill friends and how, if that's the case, they should be killed instead. She reaches into her purse and comes up with a heavy, sharply pointed pair of scissors and hands them to Deuce.

She tells him to take the scissors apart, give her one blade and take the other. "We'll wait in the lounge. When they come in the lobby, I'll go up to Chucky and he'll never expect it—like I'm going to give him a big kiss or something—and I'll stick him."

Deuce is angry that Karyne isn't already packing, but he's impressed too. He has had girlfriends who wanted to kill him, but none who ever offered to kill *for* him. He says nothing for a moment, then tells Karyne they can leave Dallas together or she can stay, in which case she will die. Less than twenty minutes after Chucky's phone call, they are back on the road together.

CHAPTER 48

KARYNE AND DEUCE DRIVE FROM DALLAS TO LAS VEGAS IN ABOUT twenty hours, popping black beauties to keep themselves awake. It's a hard and panicked trip, all 1,215 miles of it. They go northwest out of Dallas, across the southwestern edge of Oklahoma, then straight across the stark, sere plains of the Texas Panhandle, stopping for gas whenever necessary, and taking the shortest of breaks in Amarillo on Interstate 40. They stay on the interstate all the way and, except for a break in Albuquerque, push across the blurred green and tan of New Mexico, then on and into Arizona, where the remarkable red-rock beauty of the land is lost on them. They make a harried pit stop in Flagstaff, halfway across the state. The final leg along Interstate 40 takes them to the Nevada border. From there it's just a short roll north to Karyne's place in Las Palmas Apartments, an ill-kept complex on a road with the unlikely name of Paradise.

The city's famous Strip is nearby and as busy as ever. Karyne's apartment looks the way she left it. In the kitchen's double sink sits a tangled jungle of greenery—pots of asparagus ferns, variegated coleus plants, and philodendrons that Deuce had watered before the couple left town. Karyne returns each of the plants to its customary place. In the process she notices that a screen on one of the apartment windows has been torn.

"I think somebody was here," she says.

Deuce hears Karyne's words, but they don't trip any alarms; he is too muddled by the amphetamines. He has presumed death is coming from the East, behind them, leaving Karyne and him out front with time to make a move. Never did it occur to him that Chucky's call to Dallas could have come from Las Vegas. If his head were clear, he might kill himself and save Chucky the trouble.

Deuce mumbles that they should look around the apartment. They find clothes from Karyne's wall closet in a heap on the floor. She had a modest stash of marijuana, and it's missing.

Maybe just a local burglar? Deuce is still trying to force the fog from his head, but crashing from amphetamines isn't like drinking so much alcohol that you go past drunk and on into sober again. Black beauty fog has a different kind of weight; it's slippery and elusive. Deuce is fighting for alertness and can't quite reach it. Then he picks up a sound, the hard and all-too-familiar *click-click, click-click, click-click* of leathern footfalls along the apartment walk. Chucky has come for him.

CHAPTER 49

DEUCE LOOKS THROUGH THE DOOR'S PEEPHOLE AND SEES THAT Chucky is unshaven, as hard-eyed as always, but haggard and almost unkempt, which is most unlike him. It's obvious he has been watching the place for a long time. Chucky's right hand is hidden in the pocket of his sports coat. The bellhop Ricky Purcell is with him, looking nervous. If Chucky gets in, Purcell's future will suddenly be behind him, and he probably knows it.

Deuce is frantic. He backs up to Karyne's side and says in a whisper, "Shut up! Keep the lights off. Don't answer the door. Don't answer the telephone. Don't even breathe."

Deuce thinks—hopes—he locked the door when he and Karyne came home. Now they watch in silence as the knob slowly turns but stops short of a full rotation. Chucky gives the door a hard knock, then several sharp bangs, but it's heavy and doesn't give.

"Karyne," Chucky says loudly, "let me in. I know you're in there. I just want to talk to you. I see your car out here. Come on, let me in."

Then there's only silence. The minutes drag on interminably. Deuce expects that at any moment Chucky will kick the door open or shatter the lock with a bullet from one of the .45 caliber handguns he favors when a sawed-off shotgun would be too obvious. But The Strip is nearby, and the gaiety of Las Vegas is all around them.

Chucky is frustrated. He turns to Purcell and barks, "Let's go." Then he turns back to the door and, as if it has ears, he says, "We'll be back."

Karyne and Deuce exhale, sag to the floor, and just sit out of sight for a while. They usually play the stereo, but not now. The lights stay off. The telephone rings and they let it go unanswered.

An hour passes. Deuce's head is slowly clearing, but not fast enough. He tells Karyne that if anything happens she should run to the bathroom and lock herself in—not that it would help much; death delayed is not necessarily death denied. An attacker who blows open one door can do the same to another, but Deuce feels better having at least something to say about their plight. Slowly his fog and fear turn to anger, and he wishes aloud that he had a gun.

Karyne says she has a friend named Juliano, a local hood who moonlights as a restaurant maître d', and maybe he can help. Deuce met him once, just briefly. She calls Juliano and starts exchanging pleasantries, as if she is about to make a dinner reservation. Deuce wants to strangle her. "Lower your voice and get to the point, dammit!"

Karyne changes her tone. "Juliano, we've got a little problem," she says. "Here's Dennis."

She hands the phone to Deuce, who says, "Juliano, I got some people back East who came down here to pay me a little unexpected visit, and I need something like an equalizer. You know what I mean?"

"Oh, yeah," Juliano says, "I know what you mean. I got a couple of men I can send you."

Deuce grimaces. "No, I just want an equalizer and I'll be all right," he says. "Can you handle that?"

"About ten, fifteen minutes," Juliano replies.

A man of few words, this guy. Deuce likes that, but he still worries he won't have a weapon in time.

Exactly twelve minutes later, there are three knocks on Karyne's door. Deuce cracks it open for the short length of the chain lock. Someone sticks an arm through the opening and holds out a package wrapped in brown paper. Deuce takes it quickly. The arm withdraws. Deuce closes the door and eagerly unwraps a double-barrel sawed-off shotgun and five shells.

What Deuce wanted was a handgun that would make him Chucky's equal in arms. What he has is an old-fashioned street howitzer that can blow a man in half with the squeeze of a trigger. Deuce is giddy with delight; equality is so overrated.

CHAPTER 50

FOR THE FIRST TIME IN WEEKS, DEUCE IS STARTING TO FEEL AS though he may outrun fate after all. On the other hand, shotgun or no shotgun, he is still pitted against a guy who has been his lifelong friend, and he doesn't understand why. Deuce is scared and angry, but sad too; his heart in his throat. Deuce knows Chucky's tired of his asking for more money from the heist, but figures there's got to be something else at work, something he doesn't know about. It's confusing and unnerving, but all he can do is play the cards in his hand.

Deuce turns to Karyne, his voice normal and more confident now that he is heavily armed, and says, "There's only two ways in here—that door and that window." He points the shotgun at the door. "If they come in that way, we'll blast 'em, and we're going out the window." If they try to come in through the window, Deuce says, he will kill them and he and Karyne will go out the door.

Deuce wonders if he will be fast enough if "they," meaning at least two killers, split up and one blasts open the door while the other comes through the window in a simultaneous assault, front and back. He knows there's at least one other man with Chucky. That was clear in the phone conversation they had when Deuce was in Dallas; Chucky spoke in terms of "we": "We're flying right out . . . ," he said.

Deuce is sure Chucky wasn't talking about Purcell; the kid's a hustler, but he's a lightweight not a player. Deuce figures that Chucky's "we" has to include at least one of his crew, probably Danese, because he and Chucky have been tight for years. But "we" also could mean more than two men. If that's the case, he'd put money on Skippy Byrnes. He's like Chucky's fucking shadow, that guy. When Deuce and Karyne met with Chucky in the motel in Chicago, Byrnes was there, and for no reason that Deuce could fathom.

Deuce and Karyne sit in silence through the night, dozing and waking, dozing and waking, but then finally sleeping until early morning. They are hungry and there's no food in the apartment. They hazard a peek outside and see that no one is stirring in the entire complex, so Karyne walks quickly to her car and drives off to the nearest supermarket.

She returns in less than an hour, but she has no groceries. She is breathless and scared.

CHAPTER 51

DEUCE SEES THAT KARYNE IS EMPTY-HANDED, AND HE LOOKS down at her with a scowl.

"Don't be mad," she says. "Don't be mad. I had to do it. They were following me and I see this cruiser and I pull over and I told the cops and . . ."

Deuce whips the back of his right hand across the left side of her face, and she staggers sideways.

"You dumb bitch, calling the cops! We could have done that from here last night."

"Let me finish," Karyne pleads. "You're crazy. Let me finish."

Deuce's hand is raised to slap her again, but he stops.

"Somebody was following me in a panel truck," Karen says. "I could see in the mirror there was three guys in it. I knew Chucky was one of them, and Skippy, but I don't know the other guy. I tried to lose them, but they kept following me.

"So I get scared and then I see the police cruiser aside the road. I whipped right up to the cruiser, and I got out and told the cops I was being followed."

Karyne pauses, half expecting another crack across the face, but Deuce is listening instead. She says the Las Vegas patrolman pulled the truck over and ordered all three men to get out. He frisked them to be sure they weren't armed, took their driver's licenses, and told all three to stay put while he checked the IDs.

The process takes awhile. The NCIC, the FBI's National Crime Information Center, is only eight years old in 1975; tele-communication is merely a hint of what it is today. Chucky's two passengers are Skippy Byrnes, as Karyne said; the other is Joe Danese, as Deuce guessed. They lean against the truck waiting, looking worried and dejected.

Chucky takes a seat on the curb and rests his head in his hands, feeling sick. The licenses of all three men are fakes, but good fakes. The men are more worried that the cop might find some reason to ask what's inside the back of the truck. The honest answer would be sawed-off shotguns, handguns, and automatic rifles.

Chucky looks up at Karyne and says, "I just want to talk to Denny," which still is the only name by which she knows Deuce. "Let me talk to Denny, please."

With the cop sitting in his cruiser still running computer checks on the men's licenses, Karyne spits in Chucky's face and gets away with it. He may be a killer, but he's no bully.

"I know what you want to do to Dennis and me," she says. "He told me in Dallas."

"I don't have a gun," Chucky says, tight lipped, wiping spittle off his face. "Just let me talk to Denny."

Karyne saw the cop frisk Chucky, so she believes he isn't armed, and she knows full well that Deuce is, so she agrees.

The NCIC okays the men's IDs, and Chucky starts talking to the cop . . . politely.

"Look, officer, this is all a mistake. See, I met this girl six or eight weeks ago, and I was just trying to find out where she lived. It's all an honest mistake. We've made up."

Karyne nods several times to let the cop know she backs Chucky's story. And then, because Miss Sponheim happens to be blessed with more chutzpah than anyone else in this roadside drama, she asks the officer to make Byrnes and Danese stay put for ten minutes while she and Chucky leave in her car to go straighten things out with their mutual friend Denny.

The patrolman agrees. Chucky can't believe it. He gets in the passenger side of Karyne's car, and they leave for her apartment.

As Karyne tells her story, the look on Deuce's face ranges from anger to amazement and finally a stricken disbelief.

"You mean he's out there now?" Deuce hollers.

Karyne nods sheepishly.

"I suppose you gave him a gun too so he could blow my damned head off!"

Deuce breaks open the sawed-off shotgun, slips a shell in each chamber, and flips it closed. He glares at Karyne, takes the weapon in his right hand, drapes his tan suede jacket over it, and goes out to face Chucky.

CHAPTER 52

DEUCE HOLDS THE SHOTGUN AT HIP LEVEL AS HE WALKS TO Karyne's car. There's no hesitation in his stride. He opens the door on the driver's side, sits down quickly, and pulls it shut behind him. He rests the short cannon on his right leg, both barrels trained on Chucky's stomach.

Chucky is about two and a half feet from destruction. He looks uneasy but sad, as if the tougher-than-nails gambit he has run for a lifetime has worn thin. Deuce is surprised. In all the years that he has known Chucky, in prison and out, he has never seen the man like this.

"What the hell," Chucky says to him very softly. "Why don't you put that thing down? We've both been thieves all our lives."

It's an odd, eternally Irish thing to say. Chucky gives no quarter and seeks none in return. He is not pleading. He's not trying to cut a deal or reach for the upper hand. Nor is he trying to manipulate or outmaneuver Deuce. Chucky is resigned to the moment, to whatever happens. He is saying that he accepts this life they've chosen—all of it, its past, its present, and however little or much of it lies ahead, a second or a lifetime—and so should Deuce.

The silence in the car is intimate and absolute. Chucky's eyes glisten with tears. Deuce sags where he sits, tension draining, tears dripping in small rivulets. They are embarrassed, both men equally, and they wipe their eyes dry with the backs of their hands, sniffling and then laughing lightly.

Deuce breaks the silence.

"I know you and you know me," he says. "You could have talked to me anytime you wanted to. You didn't have to talk to me the way you did in Dallas. You scared me."

Chucky tells him of the newspaper story about the Attleboro lawyer who said he was representing an intermediary seeking one hundred thousand dollars for Deuce in return for his testimony about the Bonded Vault robbery and immunity from prosecution.

Deuce pretends to be taken aback.

"You mean you were willing to believe that bull?"

Chucky nods, but then says it was Karyne who changed his mind just this morning by backing the excuse he gave the Las Vegas patrolman for following her.

"She had me cold," Chucky says. "She had me cold with the cops. You give me your assurance that you won't say anything about the robbery to anyone, and I can stop them from killing you."

Deuce swears to it.

Chucky suggests they get together that night at the Landmark Hotel, where he and Ellen have rented a room. Byrnes and Danese have rooms at the MGM Grand.

"She'd like to see you," Chucky tells Deuce. "Let's talk things out, and I'll show you the newspaper clipping. We'll get something to eat. Bring Karyne."

The reunion is like old times. Good food. Plenty of drinks. Forgotten for the moment is the reason they all are back in Las Vegas together. It's Ellen who brings Deuce up to speed on events.

She is proud of Chucky. "Let me tell you, Deuce," she says, "you've got a hell of a friend here. He's a hell of a man. When he came back from seeing you, Joe Danese was in the room with Skippy Byrnes. He told Skippy to call back East and get John Ouimette on the line. Chucky takes the phone and tells Ouimette, 'Yeah, I spoke to Deuce, and he's my friend. You understand? I'm flying home tonight, and I don't have no guns with me when I fly home either. You tell them back there that if they want him, they go through me first. You understand?'"

Chucky interrupts Ellen to say that when this has all played out and they look back on it, they'll probably find out the Attleboro lawyer was helping Providence wise guys turn up the heat on them. Make it look like Deuce is willing to rat out the gang, and one of them will kill him.

"I'd bet my life it was one of them," he says.

As always, Chucky is a lousy gambler.

CHAPTER 53

THE SUGGESTION THAT THE TREACHERY OF PATRIARCA'S MOB HAS put them in their current fix is roundly greeted with choruses of damnation and I-told-you-sos.

Deuce is incredulous, but he asks a good question. "Did any of them tough guys back in Rhode Island go see this Kelly—this attorney—or go snatch him to find out what the hell is going on?'"

"Well," Chucky replies, "they thought it could be a setup. They didn't know whether it was true or whether the law was trying to smoke us out by planting the story in the paper."

Deuce shouts, "Wait a minute! You mean they send you down to blow my head off because of a story in the paper, and now you're telling me they don't know if the story's a setup?"

"That's right," Chucky says.

Deuce is lying and doing a shamelessly good job of it.

He and Karyne got the hounds of hell pounding after them all by themselves. The entire uproar, including Ouimette's order to kill him, all traces back to Deuce's own stupidity. He had Karyne call a man names James R. Hunt, a former partner of his, and tell him some men in Atlanta were out to kill him and that Deuce needed a lawyer to help him get immunity from prosecution for the robbery in addition to one hundred thousand dollars for his help in solving the crime.

Hunt called Robert J. Kelly, the lawyer from Attleboro, and they set up the meeting with the police.

As for Robert J. Kelly, the Attleboro lawyer who claimed to be representing an intermediary between Deuce and Rhode Island law enforcement? If it were to come down to legal proceedings of any sort, Kelly would be sorely out of luck; he never was licensed to practice law in the Ocean State. Nor did he ever identify his supposed client. It's not out of question that he too may have been set up, or that he was a shill to begin with. About a month after he surfaced in the Bonded Vault case, Kelly was arrested and charged with violating Massachusetts's tough two-year-old law imposing an automatic one-year prison sentence for unlawful possession of a firearm.

The understanding that Providence's second-tier renegade mobsters would kill Deuce without knowing whether he'd even earned it leaves the Lowell Two-Spot in an ill-humor; turns him pale, in fact. Deuce knows for certain now that he should have taken his own advice from the start and stayed out of Rhode Island.

Chucky tries to perk him up a bit by idly suggesting they pool their resources and invest in a motel and lounge somewhere out West. Deuce leaps at the idea. He says he figures their remaining shares from the heist will add up to about four hundred thousand dollars. Money like that, they can parlay into something. Chucky says nothing. Deuce still doesn't get it. Does he really think this Patriarca-Ouimette combine is going to cough up more money?

"Let's pack our bags and split," Deuce says to Chucky, Karyne, and Ellen, "the four of us right here. We can make it wherever we go; you know that. We don't need those guys in Providence. I don't want to go back there. How the hell can I face them guys now that they've tried to kill me?"

Chucky's enthusiasm is fading faster than Deuce can talk. "I'm even learning how to drive," Deuce blurts out. "Karyne's been teaching me. I can drive on the highway . . . as long as I don't have to shift."

The remark strikes everyone funny, even Deuce, and they burst into laughter.

Chucky suggests they break up their little party and go over to the casino at the MGM Grand to let Skippy Byrnes and Joe Danese know that all's well in Never-Never Land.

CHAPTER 54

THE REUNION WITH BYRNES AND DANESE IS A BIT CHILLY, BUT Joe does grab Deuce's hand and tells him, "Don't ever scare us like that again, huh?" They listen to Chucky's summation of events, but neither of them has much to say to the others, especially Byrnes.

Nobody ever really seems to care much about what Byrnes thinks or doesn't think, does or doesn't do, anyway. He usually isn't asked for an opinion, and he usually doesn't offer one. He's so quiet it's easy to forget he is there, no matter where "there" is. He might as well be the wallpaper in the room.

But then, that is his job. Quite apart from whatever Byrnes is told to do as a member of the crew, he has another job entirely; it is secret and much more important. He is a cutout, a soldiering spy for *Il Padrino*, and he has been since day one. Everything the crew has done or tried and failed to do, everything anyone has said of any importance, Byrnes quietly and efficiently reports to The Man or one of his designates, Henry Tameleo or Nicholas Bianco, at The Office on Federal Hill. That's his job, and he does it surpassingly well.

Byrnes is important insulation for the boss of bosses. With him in place, *Il Padrino* won't be blindsided by any unforeseen, untoward developments. With Byrnes's help, Ouimette's efforts to assassinate Rudy Sciarra were blocked at every turn. Sciarra knew what was afoot all along. He knew where to be and where not to be, and when and what and whom to look out for. Patriarca is always there, in one form or another. If there comes a day when Sciarra has to be taken off the boards, it will be because *Il Padrino* decides it, not "that fucking Frenchman," Gerry Ouimette.

And when it came to hauling loot from the hideout on Golf Avenue after the heist, who was going to bury it somewhere? Byrnes. But he didn't bury the loot, he delivered it to the Patriarcas, with Danese's help.

"Those silver bars?" Danese says nearly forty years later. "Jesus fucking Christ. At least fifty thousand of that went to help Nicky Bianco pay off his lawyers because he was in all kinds of tax trouble, yeah."

Compared to Byrnes, Danese is a grunt in this army of thugs, a tough slogging soldier with a lot of hard, muddy road behind him. He sees and accepts things as they are, in black and white, not in subtle shades of gray, where nuance, compassion, and useless sentimentality abide. He's a pro. You hire him to do something, he does it and moves on. What you see is what you get. What's hard to understand? This isn't complicated.

Danese is satisfied with his cut of the Bonded Vault cash, even if the sixty-four thousand dollars turns out to be a minor portion of the haul. Sixty-four thousand dollars was what he was paid, so that must be what he earned. The story ends there. He doesn't expect to see another cent from the fenced valuables; that's somebody else's work, somebody else's risk, and therefore somebody else's reward. It's got nothing to do with him. All he wants is what Raymond Patriarca Jr., via John Ouimette, and then Chucky, told him to expect for doing as he was told: more jobs down the line.

But then comes this business with Deuce, whom Danese never really trusted anyway, and the Attleboro lawyer in the newspaper story, and Joe feels like he's being kicked in the head. He and Chucky have been tight for years; they've partnered on countless jobs.

At the MGM Grand casino, when Chucky tells him and Byrnes that Deuce has given his assurance that he won't rat anybody out, Danese smiles and shakes Deuce's hand, but then he takes Chucky aside and unloads his opinion with all of the grandiloquence he can muster.

"You're the stupidest motherfucker I ever met in my life," he tells Chucky. "We're in serious fucking trouble here. We took up a collection and gave this guy $9,500, but that wasn't enough for him. The writing is on the wall here. If you bring this dumb bastard back to Rhode Island, I'll kill the motherfucker. I'll put a fucking bullet in his head."

Anybody else speaks to Chucky that way, he might never be heard from again, but Chucky knows and likes Joe and takes him at face value, always has. Danese's loyalty is beyond reproach, and that matters to Chucky more than anything.

"I'm not going to jail over this fucking motherfucker," Danese says. "I'm not going to jail because of this fucking piece of shit."

Chucky takes it under advisement—"Crazy Joe" letting off some steam, that's all.

CHAPTER 55

IT'S DECEMBER NOW, AND DESPITE THE BEST-LAID PLANS OF THE police, it's not they who are closing in on Deuce but Christmas, that perversely jolly time of year when reality tends to fall short of all reasonable expectations. Deuce has longed for a good Christmas for years now, thirteen to be exact, which is the number of consecutive winters he has spent the holiday behind bars. Christmas Eve finds the couple booked into the Hyatt House in Richmond, Virginia, for two days.

They have eluded capture because they have kept moving. Police aren't looking for Karyne because they don't have her name; if they did, they could track her by way of credit card receipts. By Christmas, she has practically maxed out all her cards. So when they need money, Deuce robs some out-of-the-way mom-and-pop store, taking care not to hurt anyone, and moves on.

Two days ago, however, it wasn't a mom-and-pop store Deuce robbed but the Mechanics National Bank in Worcester, Massachusetts, with Karyne as his getaway driver. He has a fat bankroll now, and he is eager to celebrate. He wants to go out with Karyne and find a nice Christmas tree that they can set up in the hotel room, decorate, and surround with wrapped gifts for each other.

Deuce is high on the season. Karyne is not. Their relationship has been a roller coaster of emotional extremes—petty arguments, joyous moments, hateful invectives answered with punches and backhands. Karyne has black-and-blue bruises more often than not; makeup may cover most of the telltale marks, but it does nothing for the hurt. She is feeling more and more trapped with every passing day, and she wants out.

Deuce doesn't see it. Karyne is just an appendage. His focus is where it always has been, on himself. He gives Karyne money so she can buy presents for him.

He shops the way he does everything, to excess. If he sees something he thinks Karyne will like, he buys it. First a jumpsuit, then six pairs of shoes and a leather coat. At a jewelry store he narrows his selection to four rings but can't make up his mind which would be best, so he buys all four.

He returns loaded down with gift-wrapped packages and eagerly sets them out in a display on a table in their room. Karyne bought him only two gifts, a long cotton bathrobe that was three sizes too big and a cheap liquor carrying case with no liquor in it.

Deuce is hurt and dejected. He makes one final grasp at this vision of a brightly lighted Christmas tree. He has been carrying that around for years like it's some miraculous green wand that can transform a yuletide disaster into a joyous memory. He tells Karyne they should go buy a tree.

Karyne is Jewish, never thought much of Christmas to begin with, and she certainly is in no mood to trim anybody's tree. They argue. They fight. They holler at each other. Deuce slaps her around some more, and when she concedes the round, he calls her more obscene names and announces that they're going to Florida.

CHAPTER 56

THEY PACK THE CAR, AND DEUCE GETS IN BEHIND THE WHEEL. Karyne takes the backseat and sobs herself to sleep. The skies open up and dump torrential rain. Deuce is doing a fair if erratic job of navigating his way along Interstate 95 South when the car's windshield wipers stop working. He manages to steer the Dodge into the breakdown lane.

A motorist tries to help but to no avail, though he does lead Deuce and Karyne to a nearby state park, where he suggests they sleep in the car overnight. Deuce doesn't want to stop. Another motorist at the park has a citizens band radio and calls for roadside assistance for Deuce and Karyne.

A mechanic arrives, jump-starts the car, windshield wipers and all, and leaves. Deuce is eager for the road, but Karyne insists they stop for an hour because she is tired and needs to rest. An hour later, the car won't start. Deuce has a fit. He gets out of the Dodge and starts kicking it repeatedly while swearing and yelling nonstop.

The man with CB radio is still in the park, and he's taking in Deuce's antics. Deuce asks him for matches so he can blow up the car. The man suggests that instead he and his wife drive them into Durham, North Carolina, which is only about twenty miles down the road.

The Samaritans leave Deuce and Karyne at a tumbledown motel just outside the city. Deuce says he wants to fly to Florida. He'll call Ricky Purcell and have the kid get Karyne's car fixed and drive it back to Las Vegas.

Karyne's not having any of it. She says the car is a Dodge, and she will only have a Dodge mechanic work on it. Unfortunately, the nearest Dodge dealership is closed for four days because of the holiday. They have the car towed there to wait for service.

The best that can be said of the next ninety-six hours in the motel room is that neither Deuce nor Karyne kill each other.

On the first open business day, Karyne waits until Deuce is in the shower and then calls a cab to take her to the Dodge dealership. Deuce of course is furious and still steaming mad when he gets to the dealership. He picks another fight with Karyne.

"I'm not going with you," she shouts. "You're nuts!"

Deuce would have slugged her if he thought he could get away with it in public.

"I've got to get in the trunk," he tells her. That's where he keeps his .38 caliber revolver. "Oh, no," she says. "You're not getting that. Get out of here."

"I'll see you back at the motel," he says. There's menace in his voice that's unmistakable, but he calls a cab and leaves.

Moments later, Karyne calls another cab. This one takes her to the nearest police station, where she tells a burly detective that while she doesn't want to get her abusive husband in trouble she does need to get her luggage out of their motel room so she can leave town without him.

The detective says he doesn't think much of men who beat up on their womenfolk, so he gets four of the biggest cops on duty at the moment and they follow Karyne in her repaired Dodge out to the motel where Deuce is waiting.

The sight of a police cruiser with cops packed shoulder to shoulder has an oddly calming effect on him. Karyne gathers her belongings and waves to Deuce in her rearview mirror. The cops stay behind to have a discussion with "Mr. Sponheim." This worries Deuce because the ID he is carrying is for Dennis Allen, but the patrolmen never check it.

Deuce can worm his way out of most tight places, and this is one of them. In twenty minutes time, he and the cops are good old boys, all smiles and redneck camaraderie. They wish him well and are on their way.

The only convenient way out of town is by bus, so Deuce buys a ticket to Nashville; he flies from there to Chicago and then to Las Vegas. He's smug, proud of himself. All of the way, he's figuring, *Won't that little bitch be surprised to find him waiting for her?*

CHAPTER 57

NEW YEAR'S DAY 1976 FINDS DEUCE ALL SHOWERED AND RELAXED in Karyne's apartment, listening to music on her stereo and sipping a highball, waiting for her to come home, but she doesn't. Mrs. Sponheim didn't raise her to be a fool. Deuce hasn't seen her since their fight in North Carolina several days earlier. He called her mother's place in San Diego, her brother's in Los Angeles, and even her girlfriend's in Dallas, but nobody has seen or heard from her.

Karyne drove for the better part of ninety-six hours straight, not to her apartment in Las Vegas but to the safety of her mother's home. She is furious to find out that Deuce has already called from her apartment. She immediately calls the manager of the complex.

"You let him in there, and you get him out," she tells him. "I don't care what you have to do. Call the police. Call the FBI. Do whatever you have to do, but get him out."

The manager calls the police. Deuce is still lounging in his bathrobe sipping another highball when there's banging on the door. He opens it to find himself looking down the barrel of a shotgun, at the other end of which stands a serious Las Vegas Metropolitan policeman.

Deuce raises his arms instantly, and a handful of armed cops swarm into the apartment. A television camera crew is right behind them. The highball glass in Deuce's upraised hand is sweating and dripping water on him, which makes him feel every bit as foolish as he looks. The police let him get dressed, and they take him to headquarters.

They confiscate his belongings and tell him to sign for them. He has $610 in his wallet and a copy of the story about his indictment for the Bonded Vault robbery. He also is carrying two conflicting sets of identification, which is the sort of thing that usually arouses suspicion. Deuce signs his name, "Dennis Allen, Great Neck, New York."

Minutes later, the Las Vegas police bring an FBI agent in to see Deuce.

"Nah, that's not him," the agent says.

Deuce is indignant.

"What the hell did you say? What the hell is this all about? Who the hell are you?"

The agent says they're looking for a man who robbed a bank two days earlier, but the robber was clean shaven. Deuce has a full mustache that could not have been grown in two days.

Now Deuce figures he's got the edge. The cops have made a mistake. He knows his rights. He demands to make a phone call. Get lawyered up, the bastards will back off, he figures.

Bad move.

"Yeah, you'll get to make your phone call," one of the cops says. They leave him alone in the interrogation room.

Several hours pass, and the next two officials who visit are from the FBI. They examine Deuce's hands and see the misspelled tattoo, "Duce."

"Ah," one of the agents says. "Dussault. Is that your name, Dussault?"

"I don't know what you're talking about."

Deuce goes silent. When he does speak, he lies. Then he goes silent again. Then he tries to tell the agents some cockamamie story that not even he would believe.

A few minutes later, the agents hand him a Rhode Island warrant charging him with flight to avoid arrest.

Deuce still won't acknowledge that he is Robert J. Dussault.

The police still won't let him make a phone call.

Las Vegas police detectives come in and escort Deuce to another room.

Then one of the men asks, "Do you know Chucky Flynn?"

CHAPTER 58

THE MENTION OF CHUCKY'S NAME SO UNEXPECTEDLY AND SO totally out of context has the impact of a punch in the gut, and it drains the color from Deuce's face. The cops know the score immediately.

"Well, the word is, well . . . he's dead," one of the cops says. "The mob shot him a few days ago. What's your real name?"

Deuce's face is a pale blank; he says nothing.

The cops leave Deuce alone in the empty room for two hours. It's the FBI agents who return.

"Do you know Chucky Flynn? He's dead because of you."

Deuce's voice is soft, low, almost pleading. "I just want to make a phone call," he says.

Instead, Deuce is taken to a glass-walled, high-security cell with three other prisoners. Guards stationed outside stare in at him constantly.

Deuce is left numb by it all. Too much has happened too fast. There are too many pieces to sort out, too many players, but the one that concerns him the most—after himself of course— is Chucky. It's true that he hasn't heard from Chucky since their confrontation a week ago. Would the bastards really kill Chucky for not following John Ouimette's order to kill Deuce after that story came out? Of course they would. Deuce asks again to make a phone call, but he gets no answer.

The next day brings three new men. They introduce themselves: Rhode Island State Police Det. Anthony J. Mancuso; Pasquale Rocchio, acting chief of Providence detectives; and Providence Det. William B. Giblin.

Deuce is haggard and strung out. "I don't give a damn, ya know? All I want is a lawyer," he says.

"We know you're Bobby Dussault," Giblin says. "We know you did the Bonded Vault robbery, and we've got to tell you that Chucky Flynn is dead and that Joe Danese did it."

Giblin looks straight into Deuce's eyes and he does not blink.

"The people who killed Chucky will kill you too," Giblin says.

Deuce is angry now, and he figures Giblin is right. If those bastards would kill Chucky—a guy who'd been loyal for years and earned them a lot of money—if they'd kill Chucky just for stepping out of line this one time by refusing to kill him, they sure wouldn't hesitate to put a bullet in his head. Fuck 'em. They killed Chucky, he'll make them pay. He'll send the whole miserable lot of them to prison.

Deuce looks back at Giblin and says, "Yeah, I'm Bobby Dussault."

CHAPTER 59

THE POLICE WASTE NO TIME. DEUCE MAKES A FULL AND DETAILED confession on videotape, naming all the crewmembers, John Ouimette and as accomplices, the Patriarcas too. He isn't very careful to distinguish the elder Patriarca from his son. From his testimony, it would be easy to infer that either or both of them were involved in the crime, and that's pretty much the case in the months ahead whenever he discusses the robbery. What the hell, he figures; if one doesn't get him, the other one will.

On January 5, with Deuce still biding his time in Las Vegas, Providence police meet with Rhode Island State Police at the barracks in Cranston, break up into teams, and make a fast and well-coordinated sweep of the Bonded Vault robbers.

When they are arrested:

John Ouimette is sitting in the audience at the Superior Court building in Providence for a hearing involving his imprisoned brother, Gerry.

Walter Ouimette is sitting with some friends at a table in the Lee-Ray Tap at 4 Pocasset Avenue, Providence.

Skippy Byrnes is standing at the bar in St. Rocco's Social Club at 89 Fourth Avenue, Cranston.

Gerry Tillinghast is at his wife's home at 1329 Chalkstone Avenue, Providence.

The last arrest of the day gets special treatment. State police and cops from Providence and Cranston stake out the house at 35 Wells Spring Drive, Cranston.

As darkness falls, two detectives slowly approach the front of the building. Two more pairs of men come in from each side, and the first two smash open the door.

A handgun is lying on a small table by a chair. A woman is seated in another chair. The only other person in the room is a man relaxing on the couch. He quickly rises to his feet and locks his hands behind his head.

"What's your name," one of the detectives asks.

"Charles Flynn," the man says flatly. "My girl is pregnant. I don't want anything to happen to her."

Detectives recounting Chucky's arrest forty years later say it took three of them to break his hands apart so they could get cuffs on him.

"He didn't fight us exactly. He just stood there with his hands locked behind his head, and we had everything we could do to pry them apart. Guy's arms were like iron. If his girl hadn't been there, there would have been gunplay for sure. I don't doubt it for an instant."

Deuce waives extradition, and the next day he is sitting in an airplane en route to Providence when Detective Mancuso turns to him and says, "We got Flynn, you know."

Deuce scowls, stammers, and blinks in disbelief. He stares at the floor and sags in his seat, as though a whole part of him just caved in on itself in sharp broken pieces that cut and hurt.

Deuce tells himself he never would have ratted out Chucky if he'd known he was still alive, never. For one thing, Chucky would have killed him, but it's not even that. Chucky is part of him, maybe the only knowable and straightforward part. Within certain decidedly liberal parameters, Chucky is about all that remains of Deuce that is nearly honorable.

And that's sure as hell gone now.

CHAPTER 60

THE NEXT MORNING, ALL THE MEN ARE ARRAIGNED IN DISTRICT Court on charges of robbery. Chucky, having departed Walpole State Prison by walking out on a furlough, also is charged as a fugitive from justice. All of them are taken to the Adult Correctional Institutions.

The next day, Deuce testifies before a Providence County grand jury, which promptly indicts the rest of the crew: Jacob Tarzian, Mitch Lanoue, Robert Macaskill, and Joe Danese.

Tarzian, Lanoue, and Macaskill are, as the streetwise say, "in the wind"; not so Joe Danese. He told Chucky when they were out in Las Vegas that when it comes to Deuce, "I'm not going to jail over this fucking motherfucker." He means it.

Danese decides he wants to turn state's evidence, but he's no dummy. He knows he can't just up and do it unless he wants to spend the rest of his days with a target on his back. He needs permission, which means he needs to deal with the man in The Office on Federal Hill. So he calls, talks to one of Patriarca's top men, Henry Tameleo or Nicky Bianco, sources say, and explains his problem.

Danese says he is told, "Sure. None of these guys matter to us, none of them. But you've got to do one thing. If anybody takes the stand and says anything that looks like it's going to be a threat to us, you've got to testify to just the opposite, you've got to contradict them. *Capisce?*"

"No problem," Joe says, "and thank you."

It's one of those crystalline moments you only hear about, and Danese knows good luck when he sees it. *Bona fortuna!*

That afternoon he is arrested in Boston, returned to Rhode Island, and taken into protective custody.

Danese is kept in a converted holding cell on the third floor of Providence police headquarters at 209 Fountain Street, in the heart of downtown; a small kitchen has been added. With the probable exception of *Il Padrino*'s neighborhood on Lancaster Street, there's probably no safer place in the city.

Having spent plenty of time in prison, Joe is accustomed to life in a small space, so he settles in for the distance, which is likely to be long given the magnitude of the heist and its attendant publicity. He is allowed to make an occasional telephone call to friends now and then, and every once in a while, a few of the detectives take him out for coffee.

After several weeks, Joe says he's pretty lonely all by himself up there on the quiet third floor and he'd like a little company, maybe a small pet. The detectives relay the request to Colonel McQueeney, who says okay, anything to keep an important state's witness relatively happy.

Four detectives—Lt. Richard S. Tamburini, Walter Bruckshaw, Urbano "Barney" Prignano, and Thomas Keune—surround Danese, put him in an unmarked police car, and drive a few miles to the biggest and most popular exotic-pet store in the area, the Rumford Aquarium, in East Providence. The detectives are figuring maybe some fish in a small tank, maybe a turtle or a hamster.

The five men walk in and start looking around and there's this shrill voice, "Hiya, Babe. Hiya, Babe. Come on in, Pwaaak! Come on in."

The noise is coming from a handsome mynah bird in a cage near some large fish tanks. The bird is jet black, with yellow legs, an orange beak, and a yellow collar.

"Hiya, Babe. Pwaaak! What's new? Pwaaak!"

Danese is fascinated. He walks over to the cage and asks the store clerk, a young man, what the bird's name is. "That's Lewie," the kid says.

"I want him," Joe says. "How much?"

"He's not for sale," the kid says.

"I just told you, I want to buy the bird. What'll it cost me?"

"He's really not for sale," the kid says, and with that, Joe opens the door to the mynah bird's cage, takes him in his hand, and walks a few feet to a large aquarium filled with piranha, vicious carnivorous fish with razor-like teeth.

The cops are shouting, "Joe, for Christ's sake. Don't. Stop right there, Joe." They pounce on him, but not before he sticks the bird in the tank with the piranha. He doesn't let go. The bird is flapping its wings and splashing water all over the place and apparently that keeps the fish at bay, at least momentarily. The clerk hollers out, "Okay. Jesus! Don't. Okay, I'll sell him."

Joe pulls the soaked mynah bird out of the water before any harm is done, and the kid starts drying Lewie off with a towel.

"How much?" Joe asks.

"Two thousand dollars," the kids says.

"Eight hundred," Joe says, "and you throw in the cage."

"All right," the kid says. "All right. The owner's going to kill me."

The detectives bring Joe and Lewie back to police headquarters; the two seem to be getting along famously.

About two weeks later, Col. Robert E. Ricci, the new chief of Providence police, goes up to the third floor to check on the department's prize guest.

He walks into Joe's room and is greeted with a shrill voice: "Pwaaak! Fuck the colonel. Fuck the colonel. *Pwaaak!*"

Fortunately for Lewie, Ricci is not without a sense of humor. He laughs aloud, shakes his head, and moves on.

But whenever he walks by Joe's cell thereafter, he's still taunted with "Pwaaak! Fuck the colonel."

CHAPTER 61

DEUCE, MEANWHILE, IS A CELEBRITY, MARKED AND MINOR TO BE sure, but a celebrity nevertheless. He is kept out of harm's way at state police headquarters in Scituate, Rhode Island. On January 20, when he makes his debut for a bail hearing at Superior Court in Providence, he is wearing a bulletproof vest and is moved through a throng outside the courthouse surrounded by a cluster of ramrod straight, uniformed, and fully armed state troopers.

He calmly names his coconspirators, says both Patriarcas, Senior and Junior, were involved, and tells the story of how he came to town, met with Chucky and his crew, and how they pulled off the job. He is calm, clear, and speaks almost without inflection. He simply lays out a factual tale of how he led the heist.

In addition to the court's usual complement of security personnel and the Department of Corrections committing squad, six members of the state police S.W.A.T. team guard the courthouse entrances. They are dressed in black combat fatigues and caps and carry shotguns or automatic rifles.

Everyone who enters the building must pass single file through a sensitive metal detector. Eyeglass frames, belt buckles, keys, coins, pens, literally everything metallic, must pass scrutiny or be left behind. No one is exempt.

In Rhode Island it is inconceivable that any malevolent power, real or imagined, other than that of organized crime would earn such a response.

Despite all the news stories about Bonded Vault, all the official and unofficial attention paid to those involved in the heist, Patriarca has been silent.

On January 23 the Associated Press publishes *Il Padrino's* long-expected and complete denial that he, or any other Patriarca, had anything at all to do with the heist.

Deuce is only using the Patriarca name in an effort to gain more government favors, Patriarca says.

"The worst criminal can commit the worst crime in the world and then walk away supported by the taxpayers for the rest of his life just by mentioning the name Raymond Patriarca," he says.

"Newspapers need this kind of perjury to sell newspapers, and the corrupt federal officials need this myth to justify their large salaries," according to Patriarca.

No matter what Patriarca says or how emphatically he says it, the specter of his involvement hangs like a shroud over the court proceedings from beginning to end.

Selection of sixteen jurors, four of them alternates, is unstintingly scrupulous and takes six weeks. DeRobbio warns the jurors that he has a witness list that is 101 names long, and if he has to, he will have all of them testify. The point is, if you accept appointment as a juror, be sure to pack a bag.

On the second day of jury selection, Judge Anthony A. Giannini, presiding justice of the Superior Court, denies a defense motion that he order the state troopers to leave the courtroom or wear street clothes, on the grounds that their armed, uniformed presence is prejudicial.

The six defendants—Chucky Flynn, John and Walter Ouimette, Jacob Tarzian, who was eventually hunted down by state police, Gerald Tillinghast, and Skippy Byrnes—reply that they will boycott the rest of the jury selection.

Before the men are returned to prison, Tillinghast complains that in their bail hearings the star witnesses for the prosecution have said the defendants are guilty before the trial has even begun. Tillinghast also charges that the attorney general is using the troopers' presence to garner votes, and that he and the other defendants somehow are being used as guinea pigs.

Despite this bombshell, proceedings in the fifth-floor courtroom somehow continue.

At the very front of the room is the seal of the State of Rhode Island and Providence Plantations. Beneath it, Judge Giannini looks down from the bench. He is a somber, oval-faced man with a private and wry sense of humor. His knowledge of the law and ability as a jurist are as highly regarded as his hatred of the Mafia is well known. A sergeant-at-arms stands by the door to the judge's chambers.

The courtroom is not big, and each of the defendants has his own lawyer. In addition to the six-man committing squad, four armed and uniformed state troopers, stolid and stone-like, stand by a gallery of onlookers. There is never an empty seat.

Between Giannini and the gallery and a court stenographer is the prosecution table; nearest the jury sits DeRobbio, the assistant attorney general.

He is tall, forceful, energetic, and quick tempered. He is well liked, has a common touch, and, when it comes to determination, makes a bulldog look like a slacker.

Next to him sits Providence Det. Sgt. Billy Giblin. He's there because he knows the turf and all the defendants on it, and because if he were not such a good cop, he could be an effective criminal; it takes a mind. Beside him is DeRobbio's special assistant, John Austin Murphy, a young Boston College Law School grad, a lawyer for only two years but already highly regarded for his ability, knowledge of the law, and attention to detail.

They are pitted against the very best, most-experienced defense lawyers in the state. Because the public makes no distinction between reputedly bad men and those who defend them, the notoriety of their clientele rubbed off on them long ago; by now they have no trouble living inside the difference, be it big or small. John F. Cicilline, Harvey S. Brower, Harris L. Berson, Salvatore L. Romano Jr., and Paul "The Bull" DiMaio are the big five.

It is an intimate setting. The combatants watch one another sweat. They can smell one another, hear every sigh of frustration, every cynical chuckle, every puff of disgust and snarl of disagreement.

If you can't play poker for life or death, you have no business here.

CHAPTER 62

THE PATRIARCAS, RAYMOND L. S. SENIOR AND JUNIOR, MIGHT AS well have honorary seats in the courtroom, at least at the start of the trial.

First the entire jury visits the crooks' hideout at 5 Golf Avenue, East Providence, and then the scene of the crime at 101 Cranston Street, Providence. Upon returning they are removed from the courtroom before anyone can testify so that Brower and Cicilline can press two issues they consider primary.

One is the presence of the armed and uniformed troopers, which Brower says turns the proceedings into an armed camp. "What would stop these defendants from taking a hostage if no police were in the room?" DeRobbio asks.

The other is the use in testimony of the Patriarca family name, on the grounds that its reputation, according to Cicilline, would be prejudicial—this, despite the fact that the jurors are sequestered for the entire trial.

Giannini affirms his stand on the troopers' presence, saying he consulted State Police Superintendent Stone, who cited departmental policy and union regulations on the issue. What's more, Giannini says, in a pretrial poll of fifty-four prospective jurors, none said they would feel influenced by a uniformed presence during court proceedings.

Cicilline gains traction with the issue of the Patriarca name, however. After privately previewing Deuce's testimony, Giannini sustains Cicilline's objection on the grounds that using Patriarca's name would lend unwarranted credibility to hearsay. All parties agree that if references must be made, they will be in the form of "John Doe Sr.," as in, "Who collected the silver bullion?" and "John Doe Jr.," as in, "Who helped John Ouimette plan the heist?"

The jury hears testimony from a number of people who lost the contents of their safe deposit boxes. Some have filed very specific claims with the court-appointed receiver; more lost items will never be specifically identified other than, for example, "twenty-five gold pesos" or "large bag of silver quarters."

Some of the people who testify obviously paid close attention in civics class and are intimately familiar with their Fifth Amendment right to remain silent so as to avoid self-incrimination. Frank "Babe" Kowal, Jerome "The Bingo Man" Geller, and Matthew Levine, for example—all of whom are currently wrangling with the Internal Revenue Service—at one point or another in testimony take solace in the Bill of Rights.

Seven days into the trial, one of the employee hostages, fur finisher Barbara Oliva, takes the stand. Brower takes her to task because she told police shortly after the heist that she didn't see the face of any of the robbers but then later identified two of them as the "first" and "second" men.

Oliva says she didn't want to get involved at first because she was frightened but later changed her mind. She saw the second man when he entered the Bonded Vault office and then again when the pillowcase over her head was lifted to help her breathe. She had sketched a likeness of him for police.

"Is that man here today," Brower asks.

"Yes," Oliva says.

"Would you come down from the stand and identify him for us?"

Oliva walks over to where Chucky is seated, points directly at him, and says, "He was the second robber."

The lawyers launch into what stretches out to be nearly two days of loud give-and-take and outright bickering over Oliva's testimony, but she holds her ground.

Giannini volunteers that he has never had a witness who was able to give such descriptive and thorough accounts of what she had seen. The courtroom is hot and humid. The air in the packed room is stifling. Two old air conditioners cool the room before each session, but they have to be turned off when the trial resumes because they are too loud. They are turned on intermittently during proceedings so that lawyers' conversations at the bench can't be overheard.

Brower asks Oliva during her third day of testimony to don the pillowcase she had worn as a hostage, and she is visibly shaken.

"Please don't make me put on the pillowcase," she says, bursting into tears. Giannini recesses the trial for lunch, and Oliva returns to the stand directly after, still visibly upset.

Brower asks for a recess.

"I had rather get this over with," she says.

Brower persists.

Giannini relents.

Recess drags on through the hottest part of the day. When the jury is seated again at 2:20 p.m., the room goes silent for a couple of minutes.

"Where's our witness, Mr. DeRobbio?" Giannini asks.

"She is on her way up," the prosecutor says.

Moments later, Oliva returns to the stand and Brower's questions turn to the sketches she drew. He asks Chucky to stand up.

"Does his chin fit the image of the man you drew a sketch of?" he asks.

"Yes," Oliva says, "that is the man."

Brower winces and asks that the answer be stricken as not responsive.

Giannini demurs.

"Do you see a dimple in Mr. Flynn's chin?" Brower snaps. "Why didn't you draw in the dimple in the sketch you drew of the man you say was the second man?"

Oliva says she doesn't know.

Brower says he is finished with Oliva for now.

It was Chucky who told her during the robbery not to look at him or he would "blow her fucking head off."

She leaves the witness stand shaken, sweat glistening on her brow but with her chin slightly raised, resolute, as if to say, "Take that, you son of a bitch."

CHAPTER 63

THERE ARE FEW DAYS IN THE LONG TRIAL WHEN THE LAWYERS' questions don't have barbs, replies don't have sharp edges, and interminable and repeated arguments over procedure and admissibility don't tempt the least-cynical observer into thinking the entire affair might be better settled with a fistfight. The tension in the courtroom is palpable; it has been that way from the very beginning.

Most exchanges are acrimonious.

Brower: "I'll wait until DeRobbio quits smirking before proceeding, Your Honor."

DeRobbio jumps to his feet and replies, "Mr. Brower should be admonished by this court for that, Your Honor! I am getting tired of this."

Giannini: "This is an appropriate place for me to bite my tongue."

At one point, the lawyers clash over whether a witness should be allowed to elaborate on a yes-or-no answer.

Giannini sometimes has to warn lawyers to stop addressing the court at the same time, or to stop bickering and shouting at one another across the aisle.

And there is more than just talking going on across the aisle. Murphy and DeRobbio sometimes return to the prosecution table to find handwritten notes on which a friend's address is written, or their own. There might as well be a blinking sign saying, "We're going to get you. We're going to get those you love."

Tillinghast, in fact, says loudly one morning that they should beat them with a baseball bat to "straighten their heads out."

Tarzian, at another point, pulls up a chair next to Murphy and says, "Jesus, Murphy. I was sorry to hear . . . I hope it isn't true. Your sister's married to a colored guy."

"That's right," Murphy says. "You don't have to feel sorry."

"Could have been worse," says Tarzian. "She could have married an Armenian."

Years later Murphy remembers vividly how Tillinghast whispered to him, "Hey, Murphy. How's it feel to have those nigger kids running around your house?"

Despite the death of his elderly father during the trial, DeRobbio is in court the following morning. Before the jury is brought in, Tillinghast says, "Hey, Al. I hear your old man died of a heart attack last night after he got a blow job."

DeRobbio jumps to his feet and goes after Tillinghast, but a state trooper intervenes.

Paul DiMaio files a written memorandum with DeRobbio telling him that some of the defendants are asking where DeRobbio lives. He suggests DeRobbio keep his eyes open.

The law Rhode Island style—no blood, no foul.

Outside the courthouse in late June, about a dozen young people start marching before the South Main Street entrance holding signs protesting what they consider excessive state police security. They echo the complaints Tillinghast made nearly three months ago when jury selection got under way. The cops don't pay them much attention.

At his weekly press conference Gov. Philip Noel defends the heightened security as a way to prevent Deuce's assassination. He doesn't name any gunmen, but says, "It is obvious that they already have tried to kill him once.

"There are several million dollars involved," he says, referring to the stolen loot, "money that is now on the street. When you have that much money to work with, the underworld element, you know, you can spend the money to hire hit men to come in and kill these witnesses.

"Regardless of how much security you have, with that many millions of dollars in the kitty, you have a very, very dangerous situation—dangerous to witnesses, judge, and jurors.

"If you have dangerous people misbehaving and acting up in that courtroom, you have the right to put whatever kind of security is required in that courtroom."

In Superior Court defense lawyers are haggling over certain aspects of Joe Danese's testimony for the prosecution. "Crazy Joe" is a portrait of decorum on the witness stand. He is neatly dressed. He tells the jury that he decided to cooperate because he already has spent fourteen years of his life in prison. His answers are clear and direct.

At DeRobbio's request, Danese steps down from the witness stand and calmly identifies all the defendants one by one except for Walter Ouimette, with whom he had no dealings. The defendants glare and sneer but remain silent.

At the start of the midafternoon recess, as the jury leaves the hot and crowded room, Tarzian tries to resist being handcuffed by one of the men from the committing squad, and a trooper rushes to help him.

Tillinghast complains that the trooper bumped his arm and interfered with his efforts to speak with his lawyer. He says his wrist has been injured.

Tarzian refuses to return to the courtroom after the recess. Brower says the man is physically and emotionally unable to continue. He worries aloud that the state police will further harm his client.

DeRobbio suggests that physicians examine both men.

Giannini has had enough. He adjourns the session for the day.

Outside, the protestors shift their demonstration to the Benefit Street side of the building so that jurors can see and hear them when they board the school bus that returns them to the Holiday Inn Downtown where they are sequestered.

The black-garbed S.W.A.T. team takes most of the protestors' abuse.

They manage to survive.

CHAPTER 64

WHEN THE JURY RETURNS FROM ITS MIDAFTERNOON RECESS ON June 28, Deuce is waiting in the wings.

At DeRobbio's request, he points to each of the defendants, identifies them, and then notes that Joe Danese, Mitch Lanoue, and Mack Macaskill are not present but that all of them together pulled off the Bonded Vault heist.

Virtually everything Deuce says about how the heist came to pass has been heard already.

He is on the stand for six sweltering days, and most of the time his voice is clear, direct, and unwavering. The cross-examination unfolds like a gauntlet in which Cicilline, Berson, and Brower all get their licks in.

Deuce's voice finally cracks; he breaks into tears and tells Chucky he's sorry, says he believed Chucky had been killed or he never would be testifying. Chucky stares through him, his eyes cold and hard.

Deuce looks at the lawyers and says, "John Ouimette sent them out to kill me."

Chucky shouts, "No. No, that's not true."

"He saved my life," Deuce says.

Giannini calls for order and gets it, but all Deuce's psyche has been laid out for the world to see. He is a down-low Janus with two scarred faces. One would never betray a friend; the other would sell his soul and yours to save his ass. Which Deuce you get depends on which way the warmer wind is blowing.

The issue of why Deuce believed Chucky had been killed gets mired and lost in debate over the precise verbiage used by Giblin and Mancuso and the exact information given them by an FBI agent named Grant Harmon, who is said to have originated the idea. If the defense can prove that Deuce was tricked into confessing, all the charges might be thrown out or a mistrial declared. But the defense knows better than to risk everything on questions of who said what to whom and when.

And so it goes.

Karyne Sponheim holds her own over two days of testimony, but Ricky Purcell is a problem. His exclusive testimony was heavily wooed, first by the prosecution and then by the defense—in that order.

DeRobbio gets him on the stand, and when the hustling bellhop's answers are not what is expected, the lawyer asks for a brief recess. DeRobbio takes Purcell into the judge's chambers; about two minutes later, the door flies open and Purcell runs out. He tells Giannini that he had no idea Rhode Island's legal system allowed a state prosecutor to call a witness "a motherfucking liar."

DeRobbio is ripping. He tells Giannini that he may, in fact, have used part of that obscenity but never the whole of it, because he believes it's the worst word in the English language.

A bomb scare is called in at the courthouse at 2:00 p.m. on July 16. After a thirty-minute search, the proceedings resume.

After a long session in court the following day, jurors return to their rooms on the sequestered fourteenth floor of the Holiday Inn Downtown to find that some of their rooms have been ransacked and money and personal items stolen.

Judge Giannini apologizes.

As the trial grinds on through July, observers start checking the record books. Not even the successful prosecution of Raymond L. S. Patriarca had required six weeks of jury selection, and the heavy betting is that this trial will be a milestone too.

CHAPTER 65

Giannini is frustrated by the slowness of the trial, and early in August he decrees that all remaining sessions will be thirty minutes longer.

Testimony ends on the seventy-ninth day of the trial, making it the longest in the state's 336-year history.

The jury deliberates for eight hours and then returns. As each defendant is brought before the bench, jury foreman Barry Dana of Smithfield, Rhode Islands, reads the verdict to a crowded, hot, and tightly hushed courtroom.

It all comes down to this: You can get away with partaking of the last good heist if one, you kept your mask in place, and two, you had a way to make people think you were somewhere else. The first is up to you; the second is up to your friends.

Walter Ouimette is acquitted because he can prove that while the robbery was taking place he was at home with his wife.

Jake Tarzian is acquitted because a couple of friends support his assertion that he was doing automotive work for them at the time.

Gerald Tillinghast is acquitted because his half-brother, Lawrence J. Mastrofine, of Portsmouth, Rhode Island, testifies that he, Tillinghast, and another man were visiting friends in New Hampshire on August 14. Mastrofine says one of the points of interest on the trip was the Old Man of the Mountain.

During cross-examination, DeRobbio asks, "And who was the old man you saw?"

"He didn't say his name," Mastrofine replies.

The Old Man, of course, was an immense rock formation in the rough shape of a man's face, but Mastrofine mentions enough other potentially legitimate activities to offset the damning impact of his lie.

Skippy Byrnes is found guilty of robbery, kidnapping, and conspiracy. He testifies that on August 14, he helped move a boat and then worked on a dock project in Narragansett Village. Byrnes's alibi sinks when the general manager of the project testifies that the dock work was finished by the end of the first week of August.

John Ouimette is found guilty of conspiracy and being an accessory to armed robbery before the fact. His alibi depends on a multipage photocopied record noting his presence during some work for the state. DeRobbio, Giblin, and Murphy notice that one page of the record, the one certifying Ouimette's whereabouts on August 14, has a slightly different and seemingly inconsequential mechanical mark on it. It appears intentional, so they question it and persist. It turns out that the mark is a manufacturer's brand, a mechanical conceit that could only have been made by a copier that went on the market some time after August 14. The original page in question had been altered to include Ouimette's name, recopied on the newer machine, and then inserted in the file.

Chucky Flynn, who married Ellen in February at the ACI, is found guilty of robbery, kidnapping, and conspiracy because his lawyers never get to unload his alibi. Among articles submitted as evidence were head and pubic hairs that FBI personnel collected from overalls Chucky used during the robbery. Chucky is a white man with light brown hair, but the hairs in evidence are certified as African American.

The hairs easily could have come from the stolen van used in the robbery. Regardless, Brower, Cicilline, and Berson are all wound up to argue that the hairs create reasonable doubt that Chucky was ever involved.

Chucky's testimony is the last of the six defendants'.

Cicilline calls him to the stand, asks his age.

"Thirty-six," Chucky says.

"Did you rob the Bonded Vault Company?" Cicilline asks.

"No," Chucky says, his voice flat and clear.

"Do you know who did?" Cicilline asks.

"Yes," Chucky says.

"No further questions," Cicilline says, opening the trap.

DeRobbio is a bit stunned and shuffles some of the papers in front of him to stall for time. Both Giblin and Murphy lean in on him before he can rise to cross-examine Chucky.

DeRobbio asks for a brief recess.

Giannini agrees.

Out of the courtroom, Murphy and Giblin warn DeRobbio that if he continues as the defense anticipates, he'll walk into a trap: Once the possibility of different culprits is raised, by way of the African American stray hair, there is room for the defense to argue reasonable doubt.

Don't go there, they say.

Moments later in court, DeRobbio launches his cross-examination and focuses on a mere recitation of Chucky's criminal record dating back to 1963.

"No further questions," DeRobbio says.

He doesn't take the bait.

Brower rushes to the bench and asks Giannini's permission to call Chucky back to the stand.

Giannini shakes his head.

"You passed up that chance," he says. "Bring on your next witness."

"We have no further witnesses today, Your Honor," Brower says.

Giannini's stare is long, cold, and forever.

Brower turns away.

It's all over but the sentencing now.

CHAPTER 66

February is winter's hard white master and a good month for punishment.

On February 8, Judge Giannini sentences John Ouimette, Skippy Byrnes, and Chucky Flynn to life in prison for their roles in the Bonded Vault robbery.

The sentences, in tandem with legal, evidentiary, and procedural issues raised during the trial, threaten to turn the Bonded Vault case into an unending Dickensian snarl of jurisprudence that could take another decade to wind through the courts, ensnaring all the people even remotely tied to it.

Brower attacks the sentencing as draconian, fit for the Dark Ages. "There is no justification for any of these men to be put in a cage for the rest of their lives," he says.

The sentences do set a precedent for severity, and Giannini knows it. He says the punishment is intended to be a deterrent. The men will be eligible for parole in ten years or less, with additional time off for good behavior.

The extraordinary value of the stolen goods also is a factor, the judge says, but the use of weapons and the taking of hostages is an even greater consideration. He says the court believes it is doing the right thing but concedes, "I shall never know for certain."

Out at the state prison, Gerry Ouimette does know for certain. He announces to anyone who will listen, "I want all of these wop judges killed." He has a crew of at least twenty renegade criminals working for him. His word is taken literally. It goes out in a hurry.

Giannini and DeRobbio both receive death threats, and so does Barbara Oliva. State police troopers are assigned to each of them as bodyguards indefinitely, sitting outside their homes around the clock.

Chucky sends the three of them a letter in which he says that while he disagrees with the sentence, he "in no way condones any threats, whether direct or indirect, that may have been made." He says he will pursue his case through the courts.

Giannini appoints a three-judge panel to hear the defendants' lawyers make their case for a more lenient sentence.

"If they feel a life sentence is too severe, then I expect them to reduce it," he says.

They don't.

The twenty-four-hour protection details are finally stopped nearly three years later when DeRobbio personally gets the all clear from one of Patriarca's top lieutenants. They can breathe easy.

When Deuce first walked into the Bonded Vault on August 14 last year, he handed Sam Levine a small piece of paper with names on it that he had been ordered not to miss.

One of them was Michael Ross. Police find him two years after the robbery. By then he is eighty-two and three days dead. He has been shot eleven times from close range with a .22 caliber automatic rifle and stuffed in a large cardboard box that sits for three days until it's found by a woman walking her dog at the edge of a park, the Peter Randall Reservation, in North Providence. It was a torture killing—one in each hand, foot, knee, thigh, shoulder joints, then the chest. A neighbor confesses: David A. Rourke, nineteen. The case has nothing to do with Bonded Vault except that Ross was once a player who stashed money there. The kid thought he might still have some.

The trial issues are still swirling when in late 1977, nearly three years after the heist, Robert Macaskill is arrested in Leominster, Massachusetts, where he and Lanoue have been working off and on as house painters. Macaskill also is wanted for stealing goods worth nineteen thousand dollars from the Providence Civic Center in 1975.

Lanoue is arrested a short time later, in early 1978. Handcuffed and sitting in the back of the cruiser, Lanoue speaks his mind to detectives Giblin and Bruckshaw. He grouses, telling them he doesn't understand why everyone is so mad because "all we robbed from was thieves." He also wonders what happened to all of the diamonds, silver bars, and high-end valuables they busted ass to haul away, complaining to Giblin that they "never got a piece of that."

Bruckshaw and Giblin, good cops that they are, take plenty of notes to document the tirade. It isn't an interrogation, it's a monologue. Despite the best efforts by his lawyers, a judge allows his verbal diarrhea admissible as evidence.

Lanoue and Macaskill are charged and sent to the state prison to await trial, but meanwhile they file a number of legal motions for the courts to consider along with others already pending in the wake of the heist. The issues range from the constitutionally guaranteed right to a speedy trial, to jury composition, prosecutorial misconduct, admissibility of evidence, and entitlement to trial transcripts on the grounds that the convicted defendants are paupers.

Activist and nationally renowned lawyer William F. Kunstler is brought in to bolster several of the trial's contested elements, including the fairness of Giannini's sentencing. Indictments get dismissed and later reinstated. The upshot is that there is a point four years after the end of the trial at which none of the convicted men are serving time for the heist.

Police have been running Deuce around from state to state and trial to trial so that he can testify for the prosecution; if you have a good rat, you use him.

Speaking of which: On March 18, 1980, in Howard Beach, Queens, New York, where "Dapper Don" John Gotti lives, his oldest boy, twelve-year-old Frankie, is struck and killed by neighbor

John Favara when the boy darts out from behind a dumpster on a borrowed minibike.

Gotti is the rising boss of the Gambino crime family, one of the most powerful in the country. Favara puts his house up for sale. It is bought immediately; closing is scheduled for the last week of July. Gotti and his wife, Victoria, leave New York to vacation in Florida. Favara is kidnapped and never seen again. Investigators say that seven men—one of them Richard "Red Bird" Gomes—beat Favara to death with baseball bats, put his body in his car, and had it crushed into a four-foot cube.

The Commonwealth of Massachusetts, meanwhile, is trying to clean things up at the Franklin County House of Corrections back in Greenfield, where Deuce testifies against Frank Campiti; Ralph Pioggia; Russell R. Baird, the guard he suckered; and the prison chaplain, Rev. Roy Leo, who was accused of raping and molesting girls under age sixteen. Sheriff Chester S. Martin, the warden, resigns in the spring of 1977, making charges against him somewhat moot.

• • •

The saga stormed into the next decade.

Shortly after 10:00 p.m. on the night of September 24, 1980, in Los Angeles, California, Karyne Sponheim is crossing the Pacific Coast Highway at Malibu Pier with a friend. They have been on a date. She is a little tipsy but not drunk, and they are in the crosswalk when a speeding BMW plows into her. The impact is awful. She lands twenty feet away, blood and brains on the pavement in front of a California Highway Patrol cruiser. A year later, the driver, Hubert Laugharn, is sentenced to three years' probation and one hundred hours of community service for drunk driving.

In Rhode Island, Byrnes and Ouimette's relatives post property bail for the two men; they go on an extended fishing trip and are not seen again until September 8, 1981, when they finally surrender to authorities. They intentionally miss the forfeiture deadline in order to tie up the courts with subsequent pleas that they not be forced to surrender the homes they put up as bail.

That same month, at the Massachusetts Correctional Institution in Norfolk, Massachusetts, where Ouimette is sent, he is married to Allegra E. Munson, a former public defender who in 1972 was named Rhode Island Young Woman of the Year. (They have since divorced.)

In 1983 Ouimette publicly admits his role in the robbery when he pleads for a reduced sentence. A three-judge panel orders Ouimette to serve thirty years and Byrnes thirty-five. They have been out of prison on the strength of the lower court ruling but now go back to jail.

In 1984 a federal appeals court reverses Chucky Flynn's conviction, saying that the presence of armed guards in the courtroom undermined his guarantee of presumed innocence.

The state appeals the ruling, loses, then sues to have Chucky's conviction reinstated. In June the US Supreme Court agrees to hear the case and later rules that the state had a right to post armed guards in the courtroom.

In 1985 fully ten years after the heist, Chucky admits his role in the robbery while unsuccessfully pleading for Massachusetts to reduce a twenty-five-year sentence he is serving there for a different armed robbery.

Rhode Island grants Chucky parole in 1989 for the Bonded Vault sentence, but he's back in action quickly. In 1991 he is indicted with thirty-two other men from the Lowell area on charges of conspiracy, illegal gambling, extortion, and drug trafficking. Basically, he wanted to control crime throughout the Merrimack Valley. As soon as Flynn gets wind of the indictment, he disappears.

Frank J. "Babe" Kowal, who ran Tommy's Discount Variety Store at 1017 Main Street in West Warwick, Rhode Island, was one of the men on the list of names Deuce had when he robbed

Bonded Vault. Kowal ran a most successful betting operation out of Tommy's, and all of his business was cash, no credit. On October 29, 1986, a Wednesday, which was when he always paid off and collected debts, he is found shot to death with a small-caliber handgun, two in the head, an executioner's double tap.

As for Robert "Deuce" Dussault, he no longer officially exists. It's Robert Dempsey now, a name he chose because as much as he favored Karyne, he always liked Chucky's girl, Ellen Dempsey, too. They were friends, but only because Chucky liked Deuce. Deuce did a lot of dumb things, but trying to steal Chucky's girlfriend was not one of them. In fact, if Chucky had known of Deuce's infatuation, there probably wouldn't have been enough left of him to put in the Witness Protection Program.

CHAPTER 67

MITCH LANOUE IS A STORY IN HIS OWN RIGHT. AT SIXTY, A CROOK might normally be entering the twilight of his criminal career. Not so Lanoue.

Of the original Bonded Vault crew, few expanded their criminal résumé more than Lanoue. His FBI file—or, more accurately, files—was a wrist-bending 1,422 pages in length. Much of what the Department of Justice provided was redacted, possibly to protect the names of the guilty.

In 1981 Lanoue was elevated to celebrity status by the FBI. Amassing a criminal record beginning with his first arrest on May 29, 1938, for a burglary job in Albany, New York, and stretching more than four decades, the Department of Justice finally came to the conclusion he should be entered into the Bureau's "Top Thief Program." Beyond bragging rights, the distinction earned him intense around-the-clock surveillance by a network of agents and task force members including troopers from Rhode Island, Massachusetts, and local police. Lanoue had slipped through their fingers for nearly three years after Bonded Vault, and they were hell bent on making sure that didn't happen again.

The original indictment against Lanoue and Macaskill had been dismissed the year before, but behind the scenes prosecutors were working to charge him again. That alone was a good reason to keep close watch, considering his penchant to disappear, but investigators had other reasons.

A year earlier—just when Lanoue had been released from prison—a small crew of bandits knocked off a Purolator armored car in East Killingly, Connecticut. They made off with $36,400 in cash and $463,413 in potassium gold cyanide. It's likely the thieves didn't know what they had: Jewelry manufacturers use the powdery substance to gold-plate metals. The FBI's antenna went up a short time later when Lanoue and two other suspects were casing precious metal firms in southern Massachusetts and Rhode Island. Agents figured the only way the compound would score any value is if the thieves could fence it to a less-than-reputable business.

Lanoue was also the prime suspect in an armed invasion of a gold firm in Pawtucket; one of his crew happened to work at the business just two week prior to the stickup. Agents weren't big on coincidences.

His name also surfaced in the execution-style death of a local well-driller who was employed on the side as a cocaine dealer and chop-shop aficionado, who also knew a few things about moving hazardous materials long distances. Another man was convicted of the crime some twenty years later, but for now the victim's paths had crossed Lanoue too many times to ignore.

Lanoue proved to be an impressive adversary for those tasked with tailing him. Detailed surveillance logs of his travels showed he routinely made sudden U-turns or purposely headed down dead-end streets, only to reverse direction. His evasive style forced the FBI to turn to the sky in order to keep tabs. Weather permitting, they used aircraft to monitor his movements.

Lanoue and Macaskill were indicted again that December, and all of that surveillance paid off. Investigators knew just where to find him. But the government's victory was short-lived; in 1985 a judge ruled prosecutors failed to give the pair a speedy trial. Like the victory, however, his freedom was also short-lived, and it happened in classic Lanoue style.

When state police knocked on his door shortly after midnight searching for a suspect, Lanoue swore up and down that he wasn't harboring anyone and invited detectives in to clear his good name. Mitch was right: He wasn't providing cover, but the six handguns—one with a silencer—sawed-off shotgun, burglary tools, masks, wigs, police scanners, security guard uniforms, pot plants, and a copy of *The Marijuana Grower's Guide* littered throughout the house caught their attention.

The state police never could quite pin down the name of the guy they were chasing. If it was a setup, it was brilliant and played into Lanoue's weakness: impulsiveness.

The state supreme court overturned the Bonded Vault dismissal while Lanoue was being held for that embarrassing fiasco. The attorney general's office made the obvious argument that the reason it took so long to bring about a trial was because Lanoue was on the run for a few years. Both he and Macaskill finally threw up their arms and pleaded no contest to nineteen counts. Lanoue received a suspended sentence for Bonded Vault—including time he had already been in custody—but had to serve four years in prison thanks to his decision to let state police into his armory of a house.

Lanoue was released in 1990, but not for long. Within a year he was arrested in connection with two armored car robberies that snared some $320,000. His coconspirator flipped faster than a gymnast. The dean of Rhode Island's defense attorneys, Jack Cicilline, worked his magic again, convincing the jury the guns found in the affable seventy-year-old man's bedroom weren't actually his.

What appeared to be the end of the road, though, came in 1993. After weeks of careful planning, Lanoue found himself approaching an armored car outside a department store over the border in Bellingham, Massachusetts, a .38 caliber handgun tucked in his belt. Based on his past exploits, the take was going to be modest at just forty-four thousand in cash. But that careful planning had been passed off, and an army of Rhode Island state troopers and FBI agents lay in wait.

As he neared the truck, his hand creeping toward his piece, federal agents and troopers gunned their cars into the parking lot and sprang out, weapons drawn.

Lanoue almost "took a heart," which is to say, had heart attack, Rhode Island–style. Immediately knowing his run was over, the seventy-two-year-old threw his hands in the air, screaming, "You got me! I'm Mitch!" He was courteous enough to let them know he was packing heat. As Lanoue was being put into handcuffs, his advanced age weighed on him. "I'm gone for life," he said.

For what it's worth, he told police he was alone, but the story didn't stick, and two others were pinched in the raid.

Nearly two decades after Bonded Vault, the heist finally caught up to old Mitch. A state judge quickly sentenced Lanoue to nineteen years as a probation violator for the suspended sentence he received for the 1975 job. After hearing his fate, he turned around to an FBI agent seated behind him and barked, "I hope you're happy now, you piece of shit."

The tank was finally empty when Lanoue was released from prison in December 2010. A family member who took him in said he spent his final year reliving his various "crazy robbing escapade stories" to anyone who cared to listen. But of the seven decades of heists, capers, holdups, thefts, and burglaries he talked about, he never opened up to his kin about Bonded Vault.

"There was plenty of that robbery that Mitch did not share even with us," the family member said. "It was connected to very powerful people."

On January 8, 2012, one year almost to the day he walked out of prison a free man, Lanoue's heart finally decided enough was enough. He was ninety years old.

• • •

Robert Macaskill was far less bold than his friend and codefendant Mitch Lanoue, but he was just as adept at getting caught.

In 1988, after pleading guilty for his role in Bonded Vault, Macaskill was released from prison because he had spent five years—off and on—awaiting trial. Satisfied he'd already served enough time, prosecutors recommended the judge suspend the rest of his sentence with assurance from Mack that he'd behave.

Macaskill bid farewell to his buddy Lanoue and walked out of prison. Eight months later, the pair was reunited.

While free, Macaskill spotted a stunning nine-bedroom brick colonial on Providence's tony East Side. The home was perched on a hill in the shadow of Brown University, and Macaskill had cased it out, waiting for the right time to break in. His chance came after the sun went down one night in early September.

Mack knew the house had an alarm system, which made the job even more enticing: Clearly there were things worth protecting. He was a pro, or at least he had convinced himself he was. Macaskill first cut the phone line to the house, but he knew he had to work quickly once he forced his way in because he'd have to either punch in the code to silence the alarm or use another method to quiet the system. He chose the latter and went with brute force.

Entering through a window wasn't an option because that would immediately trigger a loud alarm, so he forced his way in through the front door and quickly made his way to the alarm system's control panel, opened the cover, and masticated the insides. He waited a beat. Nothing. Mission accomplished.

The only problem with Macaskill's plan was that, unlike the antiquated one-way wire that connected Bonded Vault to the Providence Police Department, modern alarm systems alert the company when the connection with the telephone service is interrupted. So unbeknownst to the forty-six-year-old crook, two Providence patrolmen were already on the way before he had a fistful of the control panel in his hand.

He might have been able to make a quiet escape; the officers would likely have walked up to the front door and knocked, giving him the chance to sneak out the back. But unfortunately Macaskill had neglected to actually close the door, so before the officers were even out of their cruiser, they spotted the shadow of a lanky figure lurking just on the other side of the threshold.

Macaskill took flight, but he made it just one street away before he was apprehended. Unlike the spoils from the heist thirteen years earlier, Mack didn't make off with a damn thing. Not even his pride.

With few legal options on the table, his lawyer cut a deal with prosecutors. Once again, however, the Bonded Vault hangover lingered, and he was given seventeen years in prison for the suspended sentence. The judge was none other than the honorable Albert DeRobbio, the prosecutor in the original Bonded Vault trial. DeRobbio had a meteoric rise after leaving the attorney general's office, eventually becoming the chief judge of the Rhode Island District Court system, thanks in part to his role in the longest, most-expensive trial in state history.

The last time Macaskill showed up on the government's radar screen was nine years after his release from prison. In 2005 Mack and a cohort had backed a truck up to an auto repair shop in Coventry and started loading old rusty brake drums quickly into the bed of the pickup. It was early in the morning, and a neighbor heard a racket, called the cops, and stood in front of the truck so the suspects couldn't leave.

Mack claimed he had permission to take the worn parts, but the business owner begged to differ.

After being one of the legendary figures who pulled off the greatest and most daring heist in state history, Macaskill, now sixty-two, was pinched for trying to make off with less than two hundred dollars' worth of scrap metal.

The courts took pity on Macaskill and gave him a six-month suspended sentence for the misdemeanor. He is believed to be still living in Rhode Island.

• • •

The government got Joe Danese the hell out of the Northeast. After he turned state's evidence, plenty of people wanted him dead. None of Patriarca's henchmen of course, because good old Joe had *Il Padrino's* back during the trial, loyally shifting the spotlight Dussault had put on the old man. But his testimony had done plenty of damage to others, most notably Chucky Flynn.

Danese's cooperation was a big middle finger "I fucking told you so" to Chucky. He had told Flynn in Vegas that Deuce was no good and needed to be clipped.

Like so many others who entered the Federal Witness Protection program, the straight and narrow wasn't for Danese. It wasn't because of money—though he didn't have any—and it wasn't for the glory of the job. It's because he was allergic to freedom, or at least the government's version of it.

Armed with a handgun, Danese held up a Virginia bank in 1998. The goal wasn't the money, it was to get caught. With a silent alarm tripped, officers had the bank surrounded within minutes, guns drawn. Danese didn't even put up a fight; he walked outside with his hands in the air and carefully put his piece on the ground.

One of Danese's former Providence police handlers was Urbano Prignano, who eventually was elevated to chief under Mayor Vincent "Buddy" Cianci. Prignano wasn't the least bit surprised by the news of the failed bank robbery. Prignano had spent so much time with Danese, part of a team protecting him during trial, that they had become friends. It was Prignano who would make a run to the liquor store on Friday night during that time to pick up a few bottles of wine and bring them back to Danese's makeshift apartment in the police department. All so Joe could romance his girlfriend—a Massachusetts schoolteacher—and relieve a little tension.

"He wanted to get caught," Prignano said. "That was his life. Some guys like being incarcerated, and Joe was one of them."

To highlight the value Americans put on financial institutions, one of the formal charges leveled against Danese for the attempted job in Virginia was oddly worded "entering a bank/church while armed." Joe was sentenced to twenty years.

His sister—still living in Joe's hometown of Haverhill, Massa-chusetts—said the family hasn't heard from Danese in years. "He's not really a bad guy," she said, adding he's probably keeping his distance for their safety as well.

When Danese squares up his sentence in 2017, he'll be eighty-one years old.

• • •

Ralph "Skippy" Byrnes has been a ghost. Either he is one of the rare examples of incarceration transforming a man or, unlike his Bonded Vault contemporaries, he is far better at not getting caught.

In 1991, with DeRobbio a chief judge in the state system, Byrnes turned to federal court for help in overturning his thirty-five-year sentence. In his appeal, Byrnes argued DeRobbio was deceptive during the trial when the state disclosed only a portion of Dussault's impressive rap sheet. Unfortunately for Byrnes, the court ruled he wasn't in prison because of Deuce's testimony but Danese's.

Byrnes's legal battle against the state proved unnecessary; the parole board released him to home confinement that same year. He hasn't been back to prison since.

• • •

If there were a Hall of Fame for organized crime figures in Rhode Island, Gerry Tillinghast would be a first-ballot selection.

A feared Patriarca enforcer, Tillinghast was rumored to have taken part in several gangland slayings, but he was convicted of just one. Fresh off an acquittal in the Bonded Vault case, Till-inghast was out for a ride in a stolen car with his friend and loan shark, George Basmajian. Tillinghast's brother Harold was behind the wheel, which was being tailed by detectives from the state police. At some point the investigators managed to lose track of the vehicle, and in that small window of time, Tillinghast pumped nine rounds into Basmajian, the last three for good measure.

Police spotted the brothers again at a Providence bar later that night and charged them with the homicide. Both men have always maintained their innocence, but Tillinghast was sentenced to life, which turned into about thirty years thanks to the Rhode Island Parole Board.

While serving time for the murder, Tillinghast was moved to a New Hampshire prison after another inmate used a homemade shank to stab him in the neck three times in the prison print shop. Correction officials said the move was for Tillinghast's safety, but, truth be told, it was probably to protect the guy who did it, as well as any of his friends.

While in New Hampshire, his stranglehold on mob operations in his home state didn't diminish. Tillinghast only enhanced his underworld notoriety when investigators tracked the leadership of a lucrative Providence bookmaking enterprise all the way back to Tillinghast's prison cell. It was a strained definition of work release.

In 2007, Tillinghast walked out of the ACI a free man— minus probation—and twenty-two months later he was back. In a sting that state police indelicately dubbed "Operation: Mobbed Up," Tillinghast was ensnared in a predawn raid along with seventeen other criminal associates. He was charged with running a gambling and narcotics ring. Tillinghast's résumé was wiped clean of the "drug dealer" designation when, in a plea deal with prosecutors, the narcotics charge was dropped. He pleaded no contest to the ever-hazy conspiracy count and sent back to the ACI for two more years.

Tillinghast was released in time to start collecting Social Security benefits. In all, he spent just about half of his life in prison.

In 2014, Tillinghast surprised many people by agreeing to an interview as part of a profile on State Police Col. Steven O'Donnell for NBC's *Today Show*. Tillinghast told correspondent

Andrea Canning that he had a seven- or eight-page criminal rap sheet but declared flatly—if not proudly—that 95 percent of them were vaporized by acquittals or dismissals.

He said that after the *Godfather* movies were released, "alleged mobsters were coming out of the cracks, but they were all popcorn gangsters."

Not Tillinghast. No one dared question his credentials.

• • •

Jacob Tarzian died in the driveway of his Millbury, Massachusetts, home. His bullet-ridden body lay for fifteen hours. Neighbors later told police they heard what they thought could be gunfire but chalked it up to a bad carburetor. One resident told a reporter from the *Providence Journal*, "Living so close to Route 20, you heard a lot of car and truck backfires." Not that anything could have saved him; nearly a dozen .38 caliber bullets had ripped holes in his chest, abdomen, and back.

It happened ten years and two weeks after the robbery of Bonded Vault. Police say the fifty-five-year-old Tarzian was returning from the grocery store at 9:30 p.m. when two men ambushed him just as he stepped from his car. Tarzian's loyal German shepherd was gunned down too—either collateral damage or the gunmen needed to take down a charging dog.

The assassination was a stunner for the former mill town south of Worcester, which saw only a handful of murders that decade. Four years later, detectives from Millbury and the state police tracked down three men; two were arrested and convicted of murder for hiding in the bushes and unleashing a hail of gunfire at Tarzian and his pet, a third for being an accessory.

Decades later, retired Worcester County District Attorney John Conte, who was a young prosecutor on the case then, said that while he could not remember the motive behind the killing, he did not think it was linked to Bonded Vault.

But if the heist didn't prompt Tarzian's dramatic end, it certainly defined him. Every article and obituary that detailed the homicide would reference the robbery within the first few paragraphs, if not the first sentence.

Tarzian and the others would forever live and die in the shadow of Bonded Vault.

CHAPTER 68

CHUCKY FLYNN HAD KEPT HIS MOUTH SHUT FOR MORE THAN a decade, and he was finally able to collect his reward. He had remained silent throughout the trial and, while behind bars, never dimed out his coconspirators or anyone else linked to the Bonded Vault case. Patriarca died in 1984, and his son was now in power. The blessing came from Federal Hill: Flynn could take over the rackets in the Merrimack Valley of Massachusetts and New Hampshire.

Chucky was home.

While his base of operations was over the border in New Hampshire, he ran everything and anything in Lowell, right where he and Deuce had cut their teeth. Within two years of his release from prison, Chucky had strong-armed control and built up an admirable criminal empire.

In underworld circles Chucky was a celebrity now, and his penchant for violence swelled to legendary status. State investigators caught him on a wiretap telling one of his soldiers to make sure a client made good on a payment. "You just tell him, I don't hear no fucking stories," he said. "You've got to pay something." His loan-sharking operation was charging a modest 260 percent APR.

State police investigators conducting surveillance on Flynn noticed an impressive and distinct trait with the Merrimack Valley gangster: He went right around the underboss in Boston and reported directly to Providence. One of those working a case against Flynn was Det. Lt. Mark Delaney, who would later rise to lead the Massachusetts State Police as colonel.

Delaney said Flynn was the first person they had ever seen who had direct access to Federal Hill. There was a hierarchy after all, a pecking order in *La Cosa Nostra*, yet Flynn bypassed it all.

"Everyone else answered through the North End," Delaney recalled. "He had that status where he could report to Rhode Island even though he was operating on Boston's turf."

That status likely came with a certain level of protection from Providence. With money and communication going directly to The Hill, feelings were dangerously hurt in Boston.

But as the money rolled in, Flynn's relationship with the wise guys in Providence started to get rocky. Investigators spied Patriarca soldier Robert Deluca meeting with Flynn at Rockingham Park racetrack in Salem New Hampshire. Detectives said it was to iron out differences in the gambling operation. More money had to move south.

By 1991 law enforcement had Flynn good, indicting him as the ringleader in an eight-million-dollar gambling and loan-sharking operation.

They had barely scratched the surface.

Flynn disappeared as soon as he got wind that thirty-two people, including some of his best bookies, loan sharks and associates, were getting scooped up in a predawn raid. Deluca was brought up from Rhode Island to face charges courtesy of the visit he paid Flynn at the horse track.

While Chucky was on the run, FBI agents continued to turn over stones in his criminal syndicate. The breadcrumbs led over the border to New Hampshire, where the Feds learned Chucky and a crew of five had knocked off armored cars, supermarkets, and banks, including a $250,000 haul from First New Hampshire Bank in Stratham.

Several months after the indictment, Delaney got wind that Chucky was going to be at a Dunkin' Donuts shop on Winter Hill in Somerville, Massachusetts. The detective's source said Flynn was there to settle up some business before he left town again. It was a short window and a rare opportunity to get a high-priority target. Delaney called Det. Lt. Ed Davis of the Lowell police, with whom he had been working the case. Davis would later become commissioner of the Boston Police Department and a national figure after the 2013 Boston Marathon bombing.

The men left early because they wanted to scope out the Dunkin' Donuts to know where to position their team of troopers and detectives to move in and take Chucky down. Davis was behind the wheel of a beaten-up unmarked sedan they had seized from another case; one of his detectives, Robert DeMoura, was in the back, and Delaney sat in the passenger seat. As they approached the parking lot, Delaney spotted a car backed into a space in the lot with a familiar face behind the wheel.

"Eddie," Delaney said. "That's him; he's here already."

Flynn was a full three hours early, and the small army they had planned to make the arrest wasn't even close to being in position. Delaney figured Flynn was doing exactly what they were: scoping out the scene, just in case things went wrong. Davis kept driving past the Dunkin' Donuts and looped around the block as they decided what to do. Three against Flynn was far less than ideal.

"He's right there. We can almost touch him," said Delaney.

Waiting to get a team in place might be safer, but the men decided it could take too long, and there was no fucking way they were letting him slip away again. Delaney suggested they pull in and park like three guys going to grab a cup of coffee, then make their move as soon as they were all out of the car.

Maybe it was the adrenaline of the moment or Davis had a last-second change of plans, but there was nothing casual about their entrance into the parking lot. Davis gunned the engine, and its crappy suspension bounced as they peeled into the parking lot, sending the car airborne. They came to a screeching halt right in front of Chucky's car. DeMoura sprang from the backseat clutching a small shotgun and leveled it at Flynn's head. All three were in plainclothes.

Flynn could easily be forgiven for turning a bit pale. His first thought was that this was a mob hit, and, unlike all the ones he had done for the mob in the past, this time he was the target.

It didn't take long, however, for Flynn to recover.

"Chucky Flynn?" Delaney asked.

"How about those Red Sox," Flynn said calmly. "They going to win this year?"

"You are Chucky Flynn, right?"

"Do you think they have a shot at the World Series?"

Later on Flynn figured out Davis was from his old stomping grounds. He flashed a huge smile and said, "Hey! Lowell. Great to see you," then started asking about how some of the cops he knew were doing.

It was October in New England, but Chucky was sporting a healthy tan. Delaney was able to figure out Flynn had spent his time out on the West Coast in California. What he was doing out there they didn't know and frankly didn't care. "I was less interested as to where he had been as to where he was going to be," Delaney said years later.

While he was on the run, a second indictment had come down, this one out of New Hampshire. Once again Flynn was poised to make legal history: It was the first-ever federal RICO case the Granite State had ever seen. New Hampshire didn't have a legacy of mob bosses.

In the end a jury found Flynn guilty of fifteen counts, including bank robbery, racketeering, extortion, threats, and firearms charges. Three days before Thanksgiving 1992, he was sentenced to a soul-crushing 562 months in prison. Unlike his time in Rhode Island's state prison system, the federal government didn't offer parole, which meant, at fifty-one years old, Chucky would have to serve every minute of the forty-seven-year sentence.

• • •

Emotionally speaking, Flynn wasn't chained to anything. Legally he and Ellen were still married. But right before the indictment, Ellen finally cut the cord to the relationship. As the pressure mounted from running a multimillion-dollar criminal operation, Flynn's gambling had gotten horrific, and he was becoming increasingly abusive. Ellen shed herself of his identity and stole away with her two boys—both fathered by Chucky—to seek shelter.

Over the years Flynn had earned millions of dollars through his various criminal escapades, but much of that was lost thanks to his searing gambling addiction and legal bills. Ellen and the kids didn't see much of that cash; while he was serving time for Bonded Vault, the family lived in the projects of Charlestown and Woburn, Massachusetts. When he took to the wind to avoid his arrest, it was the last time Chucky ever saw his wife and kids.

On October 1, 2001, Chucky Flynn died in federal prison, the high-security supermax in Lewisburg, Pennsylvania. A report from the Department of Justice states the cause of death as liver failure. For decades Chucky dealt with hepatitis, which he insisted he got from the needle used while getting an ill-conceived prison tattoo. Jails were not exactly dens of cleanliness. Flare-ups would occasionally force him into segregation while behind bars and require isolation from his family when on the outside. In the end, Chucky started turning yellow, and his liver finally gave out.

His heart, of course, had been shattered decades earlier.

Those close to him say Chucky never got over Deuce's disloyalty.

"Bobby was his best friend," one said. "He loved him."

CHAPTER 69

It's July 17, 1982; Karyne Sponheim is nearly three years dead, and Chucky Flynn is still in Rhode Island seething over Dussault.

But in mile-high Denver, Deuce has other things to worry about.

Deuce's three children by two former wives and his thirteen brothers and sisters, including the sister who was in reality his mother, haven't seen him since long before the Bonded Vault heist nine years ago.

Worse yet, he is still estranged from Chucky—the man he unwittingly, at least at first, betrayed; the one person in his life who really ever meant anything to him; the man who now, in a heartbeat, will blow his balls off with his shotgun if only given a second chance.

But Deuce is nothing if not a survivor, and to survive he knows he must move on. So move on he does; beyond the mourning of Karyne's passing, beyond the lost contact with his ex-wives, his children, and all his other blood kin.

Despite all of these losses and regrets, Deuce's life—in the ways that mostly matter to him—is still good.

Thanks to the Federal Witness Protection Program, and the second chance it gave him, Deuce is still doing what he knows God always meant for him to do: steal stuff. He's still robbing banks, he's still pulling off spectacular coin shop heists, and the money, some really, really serious money, still keeps rolling in.

But Deuce, as always, is also spending as fast as he can steal, and so the beat goes on. And on this day it takes him to Klaus Degler's coin emporium at 538 South Broadway—the Rocky

Mountain Coin & Stamp Exchange. The emporium was a mecca for high-end collectors, including future US President George Herbert Walker Bush.

Deuce's sidekick on this heist is Thomas Gage, a thirty-one-year-old wannabe big-time stickup artist who Deuce has reluctantly taken under his wing.

Tom's enthusiasm for thievery is commendable, but in all other ways he is everything that Deuce is not. He's jittery and hotheaded, but Deuce attributes the former to inexperience and figures he can control the latter.

Besides, there hasn't been much for him to pick from since he held his nose and took a job at a Coors beer plant at the behest of his federal marshal handlers. The marshals vow, despite all odds, to keep him alive.

To Deuce their promise of protection is laughable.

He figures he's as good as dead if he does what the federal marshals want, and that's stay on the straight and narrow. A working stiff anywhere on God's green earth doesn't stand a chance against Raymond Patriarca's hit men, much less Chucky's vengeance.

There is no doubt in Deuce's mind that Chucky will track him down. This time there'll be no fast-talking Chucky out of it, and . . . oh, my . . . it won't be pretty.

Deuce needs to build a wall between himself and the mob, and that wall will cost lots and lots of money.

Short of somehow convincing Patriarca and Chucky that he's already dead, he needs to find a galaxy far, far away—and that's a trip that will cost him not a small but a very, very big fortune.

Turn the clock back a decade and there'd be no problem. With Chucky at and on his side, anything was possible.

But now, with Chucky soon to be unleashed and on the hunt, Deuce has to settle for just another one of the buffoons who have always been the bane of his criminal existence.

Hence his gamble on Tom Gage. The guy is no Mitch Lanoue or Bobby Macaskill, but he's no better either. Worse still, unbeknownst to Deuce on July 17, 1982, Gage is trigger-happy.

CHAPTER 70

WHAT PISSED OFF DEUCE MOST AS HE RELIVED THOSE BIZARRE thirty-five minutes at Klaus's Rocky Mountain Coin & Stamp Exchange, was Gage's lack of attention to detail.

His instructions to Gage were quite specific: First, take Klaus and anyone else in the shop into the bathroom; second, make sure Klaus doesn't go near any alarm; and third, gag them and tie them up nice and tight until it's time to relieve Klaus of all the goodies in his display cases.

Deuce figured those instructions were simple enough, even for his newly minted accomplice. But Gage had missed on all counts.

Not only did Klaus manage to trip a silent alarm as Gage was leading him away, he also managed to maneuver Gage to a back office instead of the bathroom, where Klaus had long since stashed one of two revolvers for just such an occasion.

And as for Gage's failure to follow Deuce's third instruction, well, that's the one that eventually would prove to be the killer, the one Deuce would later see as the root of the fiasco.

Truth be told, however, Deuce also had to admit his own failure to take notice that his robbery victim was wearing cowboy boots. Although a seemingly minor detail at the time, it was one that would haunt him the rest of his life.

What Deuce had learned on his previous sojourns out West is that you should at all cost avoid messin' with anyone wearing cowboy boots—trouble being that people who wore cowboy boots often saw themselves as cowboys.

Klaus Degler, in particular, had just such a mind-set. He also had those two .38 caliber revolvers to go with it.

As Klaus later tells it, he was dumbstruck when Gage started hog-tying him in his office while Deuce emptied his display cases.

The "friggin' idiot" was wrapping his hands with electrical tape over his cowboy boots, so all Klaus needed to do later was slip out of his boots to get free and reach for one of his guns.

But even for a cowboy, it struck Klaus as unwise to make his move too early. He didn't want to take a chance with his wife and one of his customers in the line of fire.

Besides, since he had already secretly tripped the silent alarm, all he really needed to do now was wait for the cops to arrive.

That's when the thunder rolled twice for Klaus.

With sirens still wailing and two cops brandishing their .45s as they burst into the storefront, Deuce looked up with a slightly bored but embarrassed expression.

Klaus couldn't help but admire the ice in the robber's veins as Deuce, without missing a beat, leaned nonchalantly against the display case.

Sorry to trouble you boys, Deuce told the cops, but I guess I must have tripped the alarm by mistake. Klaus would have cursed the two cops then and there if Gage hadn't slipped back into his office and threatened to blow his head off if he opened his mouth.

After a bit of small talk and a few chuckles, the cops assured Deuce it was no bother at all and quietly went on their way.

Klaus was seething. The fuckin' display cases were in disarray, emptied of everything save items that Deuce had deemed of little value. The cops, he figured, had to be in on it in some way. It was some kind of setup.

Deuce, meanwhile, was furious as well, but at Tom Gage. After the cops had left him to finish the heist they had so rudely interrupted, he took time to berate his protégé in no uncertain terms.

Klaus had finally had enough. He decided it was time to stop listening to all this bickering and take things in hand. If the cops weren't going to stop these characters, he'd do it himself—with one of his .38s.

But when he peeked into the storefront from his back office a few minutes later, Deuce was nowhere to be seen. Must have left in a huff, he figured, to load more of the swag into a getaway car.

Once again, Klaus decided to hold his fire. Might as well wait till the iceman returned before making his move.

Only Deuce never did come back. He'd apparently had enough of what he came for and figured there was no percentage in continuing to babysit the incorrigible Thomas Gage.

CHAPTER 71

THINGS WOULD HAVE WORKED OUT OKAY IF KLAUS HAD ONLY been a better shot.

But Klaus managed to hit Gage only twice that day in the Wild West shootout at his coin emporium and failed to kill him, which was much to Klaus's regret and Deuce's later chagrin.

Klaus Degler's first bullet hit Tom Gage in the left arm, the second in the thigh.

Not bad, Degler figured, for being out of practice for more than a decade.

As a medic in Vietnam, Degler had been wounded himself—four times—so he could tell pretty quickly that his first volley hadn't quite done the job.

Although Gage staggered and slouched against the display case as those first bullets hit, he somehow managed to keep his grip on his own gun and, to Degler's great disappointment, seemed still quite capable of using it.

But instead of firing back, Gage ran or, more precisely, Degler recalls, limp-ran out of his store.

So what was Degler to do next?

On the one hand, he didn't know whether the man he would later know as Deuce was coming back. If he did, he'd be outgunned.

But the adrenaline was pumping, and he was really pissed. He had no intention of letting the bastard get away.

Though he didn't know it at the time, Degler needn't have worried about Deuce's return.

Deuce, after all, was no Chucky Flynn, who would never leave a partner in crime in the lurch, no matter how incompetent or deserving of abandonment that partner might be.

Nor, for that matter, would Chucky ever let anyone trick him into ratting anyone out, as Deuce had done to him.

Deuce and Chucky may have long ago been minted into one coin, and in many ways still bound and inseparable, but they were also clearly the flip sides of that same badly tarnished coin.

Deuce's criminal code of honor was flexible. Chucky's was not.

Chucky's code might require that he now kill his best and, for that matter, only real friend; but he would never, ever, even now, testify against him.

Fortunately for Degler, it was Deuce, who always carried his gun just for show, and not Chucky, a crack shot with more than a few dead bodies behind him, that he now had to worry about.

With his wife and his customer still bound and gagged in the back office, Degler, against what he would later admit was his better judgment, decided to follow Gage into the street. And that's when Gage opened fire.

CHAPTER 72

In retrospect, Deuce figured things actually would have worked out just as well even if Gage had been the better shot. After all, he really had two dogs in this midday gunfight on Denver's 500 block of South Broadway.

In the long run it wouldn't have made much difference to him which one bled to death on the sidewalk that day, as long as one of them did. Still, years later, Deuce had to admit he was so pissed at his partner that, push come to shove, he likely would have been rooting for Degler.

Though the bad guys had always worn the white hats in Deuce's upside-down world, he had to grudgingly admit that Degler was really just the innocent, law-abiding victim in all of this.

Whether he was woozy from loss of blood or just a lousy shot, Gage managed to get off only five more rounds before dropping his emptied gun and limp-running off.

Much as he wanted to, Degler hadn't yet shot back.

Unlike Gage, he didn't want to risk hitting any bystanders. Besides, his daughter was at her ballet class in a building at the end of the street, and he wasn't about to take even the slightest chance that he might hit her if he missed.

Instead he dashed down the street after Gage, tackled him, pinned him to the ground, shoved his revolver into his mouth, and told him he was going to blow his head off.

Had it been Deuce with the gun in his mouth, there was always a chance he might have talked Degler out of pulling the trigger.

But Gage was no Deuce, so he opted instead for begging: "Don't shoot! Please! Please! Just don't shoot," he pleaded.

When the cops arrived moments later, Degler's gun was still in Gage's mouth.

"Get down! Down! Get down! Get down!" one of the cops yelled. Degler did, with a quickly shouted coda: "Hey, guys, I'm the one who's the victim here."

CHAPTER 73

WHAT GOES AROUND COMES AROUND, AS DEUCE WAS ALWAYS quick to say, so it really didn't surprise him all that much when Gage, still nursing his wounds, told Denver detectives that the man he knew only as Robert Dempsey was the man who had planned the heist at Degler's coin shop.

To the Denver dicks, the name Dempsey meant nothing; but to the federal marshals assigned to protect him, and who had agreed to let him go by that name, it meant way too much.

It was clearly not cool, as law enforcement authorities would learn years later while protecting the notorious Boston gangster Whitey Bulger, to have your key informant running around the country committing major felonies.

But as embarrassing as it was, and unlike what the FBI failed to do with Bulger, the federal marshals decided they had to do something to try to stop or, at the very least, slow down Deuce's crime spree.

Once the Denver police started talking to the FBI, it didn't take long for the federal marshals to know where to find Deuce, aka Robert Dempsey. After all, they had just bought him a plane ticket from Minneapolis to Rhode Island so he could testify against Mitch Lanoue and Robert Macaskill in their long-delayed Bonded Vault trial. All they had to do now was wait for him to pick up his boarding pass at the ticket counter.

CHAPTER 74

EVEN AFTER ALL THESE YEARS, IT'S STILL UNCLEAR JUST HOW FAR federal officials went to protect Deuce, or just what he gave them in return.

Documents requested under the federal Freedom of Information Act show "no disposition" in his file under the alias "Robert Dempsey" for the robbery at Degler's coin shop. "No disposition" is bureaucratic-speak for "got away scot-free."

One thing is clear, however, and it's that Deuce's crime spree didn't stop after the federal marshals picked him up at the airport in Minneapolis.

Deuce's now unclassified FBI file shows him escaping from a state prison in Canon City, Colorado, on October 28, 1985; twenty-one days later he was robbing a bank there. How many other robberies he may have committed that year, state and federal authorities are either unable or unwilling to say.

And, however unlikely, how many other robberies he committed after he was officially declared dead on October 3, 1992, also remains an open question, at least as far as his sister, Dorothy "Dot" Cameron, is concerned.

Whether it was Deuce, his ghost, or, perhaps more likely, a figment of her imagination, Dot swears on her mother's soul that she saw Deuce at his mother's funeral and briefly chatted with him, more than two years after prison officials in Minot, North Dakota, claimed he had died of a heart attack while in their custody.

Deuce, who was fanatic about keeping himself in shape, would have been fifty-one years old at the time.

Would a federal government or state agency ever fake a death to protect a valued snitch? After all, FBI handlers had looked the other way for years while Whitey Bulger ran a ruthless criminal organization. But faking a death would take it to another level.

But to the reporters who had interviewed him numerous times, and at great length, shortly after the Bonded Vault heist; who had stayed in contact with him through the years he was bouncing from prison to prison and, unbeknownst to them, still robbing banks and ripping off coin dealers; who, joined by other reporters four decades later, still felt compelled to answer so many still-unanswered questions about his last great heist; to them Dot's claim that he was still alive continued to nag.

Crazy as it seemed, they figured it wouldn't hurt to spend a bit more time just to be certain they had left no stone or, if need be, no grave unturned.

For one thing, Deuce's kin appeared genuinely shocked when two reporters first showed up at their doorsteps in Lowell, Massachusetts—more than seventeen years after Deuce had officially "died"—to see if they could fill in details about Deuce's early life.

"Dead? The bastard's dead? No way," his brother declared.

"Hey," he shouted to his wife in their house. "These guys are saying Bobby's dead."

"No way!' his wife shouted back from inside the house.

How was it possible that no one in the federal marshals service or, for that matter, anyone at the federal prison in Minot, North Dakota, had ever told any of his many brothers and sisters, or even his mother, that Deuce not only was dead but had been in the ground for seventeen years?

Was it just some bureaucratic screwup that no one ever bothered to tell them?

But a few weeks later, even when presented with a copy of Deuce's death certificate, the family was still skeptical.

"When did they say Bobby died?" his sister Gert asked.

"October 3, 1992."

"No, that's impossible," said Gert. "Dot saw him at Betty's (his mother's) funeral."

"When was that?"

"1994."

CHAPTER 75

DEUCE'S BODY, ACCORDING TO PRISON RECORDS, WAS SENT TO THE Thomas Larson Funeral Home, 21 Third Avenue SW, in Minot, North Dakota.

Wes Burkant, director of the funeral home, handled the arrangements. He picked up the body at the prison on October 3, 1992, and buried it two days later at Rosehill Memorial Park.

The bill came to $1,888. The price included a casket but no headstone and was paid for by the Federal Bureau of Prisons. No one attended the burial.

And if anyone ever needed proof that this was so—whether it be a family member or friend, perhaps even someone like Chucky Flynn—the funeral director even went through the trouble of videotaping the burial.

When the reporters asked one of his assistants later if they might see the videotape, the assistant apologized. Afraid not, she said; it had been destroyed in a fire years ago.

Two days later the director of the funeral home called back to Rhode Island. That burial videotape you were asking about, he told a reporter (the one that no family, friend, or foe of Deuce's had seen in seventeen years) was actually the only one that had survived the blaze. And, yes, he'd be happy to make a copy and send it along.

. . .

Burkant, the funeral director, did a tasteful job. A small spray of flowers sits atop a pedestal beside a casket. The camera pans to the occupant's face, changes angle, and zooms in tight: receding black hair, bushy eyebrows, thick mustache tinged with red, a broad face. In the next scene the light changes from somber warm interior to harsh bright exterior, though the tight shot is the same. In daylight the corpse looks whiter. The lens zooms back, taking in new surroundings—a broad span of lawn at a far edge of the cemetery at Rosehill Memorial Park, some leafless trees in the background.

The grave has already been dug, a dark pit cut into the earth so precisely that a huge cookie cutter might have done it, just reached at least six feet into the ground and plucked out a perfect rectangle of green lawn and gray-brown dirt. An open concrete chamber is in place at the bottom. It isn't a vault, which would seal the casket from the elements; the proper term is a concrete burial enclosure, which is cheaper and intended only to prevent the earth above from sagging into the refilled grave as the corpse decomposes. The casket rests at ground level. It is cradled in two wide belts that stretch across the grave from the sides of the lowering device, a rectangle of round rails set on a perimeter of wooden planks.

Burkant is tilted forward against the wind, which buffets the camera and leaves a muffled walloping sound on the tape as constant background noise. The casket stays open, as if the corpse inside is supposed to be paying attention while his last rights are read aloud from a well-thumbed Bible for a few minutes: " . . . Earth to earth, ashes to ashes, dust to dust. . . . Blessed are the dead who die in the Lord . . . that they may rest from their labors. . . ."

Burkant closes his book, bends over, latches the casket shut. A workman in a blue fleece jacket starts the casket rocking ever so gently from side to side as it slowly ratchets downward until it rests inside the chamber.

"Same color as the concrete, isn't it?" he says.

Burkant is silent.

The workman saws the belts back and forth repeatedly until they are free of the casket's weight. Then he rolls up the belts and removes the rails so that only the rectangle of boards remains to frame the grave. The camera lingers uncomfortably on the closed casket just before it's lowered to the bottom of the chamber, and then, inexplicably—and at precisely the wrong juncture—there is an abrupt break in the film. "Wrong" because, if the entire burial is nothing but a sham, it is at precisely that point that Dussault would do his Lazarus number. One of the biggest and most effective liars ever to strut down the boardwalk of organized crime would pop the casket lid open, climb out of the grave, and fade into permanent, government-guaranteed anonymity.

The tape resumes and the workman reappears, guiding a self-propelled hoist from which a concrete slab is suspended from four chains. The hoist lowers the slab onto the concrete enclosure, and the casket fades into the deep black forever. The cover is slightly askew, so the blue-jacketed workman uses a long-handled spade to pry it into position. When the chains go slack, he jumps into the grave, unhooks them from the slab, and scampers out.

Burkant sets a copper-plated plaque beside the grave. When the hole is filled, the sod replaced, and the trappings of burial taken away, the plaque will be staked flush to the ground so that no one will ever have to stop or even slow down in order to mow the lawn. After a single season of growth, the grass will almost cover the marker completely. In two, it won't be visible at all.

Without a burial chart delineating the occupants of the cemetery, no one would even know that a grave is there, or that in it, six feet down, supposedly lies a man's remains. Even if people were to trip over the plaque, they would find that it reads, "Robert Dempsey 1940–1992."

Is Robert Dempsey, aka Robert Dussault, aka "Deuce," really in that grave?

The reporters are all but certain he is.

But it won't be there in Minot, North Dakota, where he'll be remembered, if he is remembered at all. It's in Providence that Deuce still lives. At least in legend.

That's Providence for you. Anything can happen in Providence.

EPILOGUE

AFTER THE LONGEST AND COSTLIEST TRIAL IN RHODE ISLAND history, only three of six original defendants—John Ouimette, Ralph "Skippy" Byrnes, and Charles M. "Chucky" Flynn—were convicted for the robbery at Bonded Vault. Each was sentenced to life in prison, but within fifteen years all were released after numerous appeals.

Most of the key figures in the Bonded Vault heist and its aftermath are now dead.

Gerard Ouimette, the notorious gangster who planned the Bonded Vault heist from his prison cell but was never charged with the crime, died in a Butler, North Carolina, prison while serving a life sentence for a multitude of violent crimes. Official cause of death: lung cancer. He was seventy-five.

Charles "Chucky" Flynn died in prison on October 10, 2001—Robert Dussault's birthday—while serving time for an unrelated crime. Official cause of death: liver failure. He was sixty-one.

Robert J. "Deuce" Dussault died in prison in 1992 while in the Federal Witness Protection Program, according to federal authorities. Official cause of death: heart failure. He was fifty-one.

Raymond L. S. Patriarca was never charged in connection with the crime, but Dussault's revelations dealt a blow to his criminal empire from which it never recovered. Patriarca died of a heart attack at his mistress's home in 1984. He was seventy-six.

Retired Rhode Island State Police major Lionel "Pete" Benjamin, whose work led to the identification and eventual arrest of the Bonded Vault gang, died in 2008. He was seventy.

Retired Providence police detective William Giblin, who played a key role in tricking Dussault into confessing to the crime, died in 1996 after joining and later retiring from the Las Vegas, Nevada, Metropolitan Police Department. He was sixty-three.

Judge Albert DeRobbio, who as a state assistant attorney general prosecuted the Bonded Vault defendants, died of a heart attack at home in Cranston, Rhode Island, in 2008. He was seventy-nine.

None of the estimated thirty million dollars in cash, gold, silver, and jewelry that was taken in the Bonded Vault heist was ever recovered.

ACKNOWLEDGMENTS

Undoubtedly, a lot of feelings are going to get hurt here. When a book covers a case spanning four decades and includes research that went on intermittently for more than eight years, there are a lot of people involved in helping see it through. Any omissions are purely accidental and come with a big apology in advance.

First, we'd like to thank our families. Tim is particularly grateful for the support of his wife, Melissa, and children, Eliza and Dylan, who never made him feel guilty when this project kept him away from home. Wayne is most thankful for the loving and steadfast support of his wife, Maureen Croteau, and children, Jonathan, Amy, Amanda, and Emily FuXi. Randy would like to thank his wife and world-traveling companion, Jane Moody.

Tim is also grateful for the support of his brothers, John and Pat, and his sister, Elizabeth, each of whom grew up with this story in one way or another.

Fewer people know this story better than Beth White, the wife of the late Jack White. She has seen this through two generations now and been a believer all along. She also gets research credit for stumbling upon a key piece of information tucked away in a musty basement box full of Jack's materials. This book may never have happened without that moment.

Countless interviews were conducted for this book, and many people helped with research. We'd like to thank Jamestown attorney and former prosecutor John Austin Murphy, the late Rhode Island district court chief judge Albert DeRobbio, whose final interview was for this project; former Providence mayor Vincent "Buddy" Cianci; North Kingstown police chief and retired

Rhode Island State Police detective Vincent Vespia; the late Rhode Island State Police colonel Walter E. Stone and the late State Police Major Lionel "Pete" Benjamin for giving reporters unprecedented access to Robert Dussault; former Providence police chief Urbano Prignano; Rhode Island State Police colonel Steven O'Donnell and his assistant Barbara Laird; former Rhode Island State Police colonel Brendan Doherty; Providence patrolman Frank Moody; retired Rhode Island State Police major Michael Urso; former Boston police commissioner Ed Davis; former Massachusetts State Police colonel Mark Delaney; Deputy Attorney General Gerald Coyne; North Providence police chief and former Providence detective Richard Tamburini; Denver coin shop owner Klaus Degler; former Providence police detective Steve Cross; retired investigative reporter Jim Taricani; former *Providence Journal* investigative reporter Mike Stanton; and former Rhode Island attorney general Arlene Violet. Thanks also to the late Attorney General Julius Michaelson; various members of the Dussault family, who welcomed us into their homes and supplied us with priceless detail and photographs; retired FBI agent and spokesperson for the Boston office of the FBI Gail Mercinkicwicz; National Chief of Public Corruption and Civil Rights for the FBI Jeffrey Sallet; Attorney Paul DiMaio; Barbara Oliva for her many interviews and wonderful sense of humor, as well as her boss at Hudson Fur Storage, Gerald Palmer, who gave us access to the scene of the crime many years later; Susan Lamkins at the Rhode Island Department of Corrections; Rhode Island State Archivist Gwenn Stearn; Wes Burkant, director of the Thomas Larson Funeral Home; the staff at the Los Angeles Police Department and Los Angeles Superior Court; the media relations department at the Federal Bureau of Prisons; and Tara Murray, the director of information services at the American Philatelic Society.

We'd also like to thank the good folks at the Providence Public Library, who know their way around a microfiche machine, as well as the staff at the Rhode Island Judicial Records Center and the clerks at the Rhode Island Superior Court.

We would also like to thank several people—on both sides of the law—who provided us with information and guidance but asked us not to identify them.

Thank you to *Providence Journal* columnist Bill Reynolds for his years of support and advice and for helping us land a great agent in David Vigliano and his associate, Thomas Flannery.

We wish to note the long line of fine journalists who covered Bonded Vault over the decades. There isn't enough room to mention them all, but notably Tracy Breton, Doane Hulick, James Rhea, Dan Barry, Judy Rakowsky, and John Kiffney. We would also like to thank former executive editor of the *Providence Journal*, Karen Bordeleau, as well as the managing editor of visuals, Michael Delaney. Thanks also to Len Levin and "The Geezers."

Tim is especially grateful for the support of all his coworkers at WPRI/WNAC-TV in Providence, including Jay Howell, Patrick Wholey, and Karen Rezendes. Several other colleagues assisted in research for a Bonded Vault documentary that aired on Channel 12: Thank you to Nick Domings, John Villella, and Ted Nesi, a great copy editor and even better journalist.

Thank you to our publisher, Globe Pequot.

To the City of Providence, we are eternally grateful for your unpredictable and never-ending supply of material. This is, after all, a work of nonfiction. You could make it up, but nobody would believe it.

Finally, thank you to Robert "Deuce" Dussault. His patience and countless hours of interviews at the Rhode Island State Police barracks, at prisons, and during random phone calls from all over the country and apparently while on the run from various crimes prior to his alleged demise, were invaluable.

INDEX

12/12/16